The Failure of Anarchism

by

Keith Preston

The Failure of Anarchism
by
Keith Preston

Copyright © 2016

Black House Publishing Ltd
ISBN-13: 978-1-910881-24-8

Black House Publishing Ltd
Kemp House
152 City Road
London
United Kingdom
EC1V 2NX

www.blackhousepublishing.com
Email: info@blackhousepublishing.com

Contents

Introduction: Anarchism or Anarcho-Social Democracy?

A century ago, Anarchism was an international mass movement involving millions of adherents. Anarchists dominated the radical wing of the international labor movement. The anarchist communities that sprang up in nearly every major city were a conspicuous part of urban life as anarchists were a visible and recognized minority alongside various ethnic and religious groups. Over a twenty year period in the late nineteenth and early twentieth century anarchists assassinated the head of state in every major country. The very term "anarchist" struck fear into the heart of politicians, monarchs and robber barons everywhere. The ruling class never knew when or where the anarchists might strike again.

A few years ago, I came across a book on the historic anarchist movement, that claimed a unique characteristic of anarchism was its utter failure to achieve any of its objectives. I had to laugh. The reality of course is that anarchism was one of the most successful mass movements ever. Yes, the state has yet to be abolished. No nation to date has adopted the black flag as its own. Yes, the international bourgeoisie retain their power. Class rule is with us now as much as ever. However, when we look at the state of things in the industrialized world a century ago we see that history has indeed moved in our direction.

Anarchists were at the forefront of the movement for the eight-hour workday. The Haymarket martyrs gave their lives for this cause. At one point it was illegal to organize labor unions. Striking workers were regularly gunned down by government agents and private thugs. It was a federal crime in the United

States to distribute information about contraception. Orphaned children were confined to slave-like conditions and used for medical experimentation along with the mentally handicapped, juvenile delinquents, homosexuals and others. Prison conditions often rivaled those of Nazi concentration camps. The death penalty was regularly imposed for burglary and grand larceny. People of African descent were regularly murdered and terrorized by gangs of racists while authorities looked the other way.

Anarchists were among the earliest and most militant opponents of all of these conditions. The eight-hour day, the right to organize unions, read sexually explicit literature, practice contraception and obtain abortions and engage in antiwar protests, prison reform and countless other rights and privileges that we take for granted today did not exist at the time of the classical anarchist movement. Roger Baldwin was inspired to found the American Civil Liberties Union after hearing a speech by the anarchist and pioneer womens' rights advocate Emma Goldman. Anarchists were among the earliest opponents of the mistreatment of homosexuals as well. In many ways, things have advanced considerably over the past century.

Anarchism declined as a mass movement largely because of the treachery of the statist left. The Communist revolution in Russia of 1917 was a seeming success for the radical workers' movement. Many workers began to drift towards Communism unaware that the Bolsheviks had stabbed the revolution in the back. The defeat of the Spanish anarchists through the combined efforts of the Fascists and Communists in the 1930s largely sounded the death knell for the historic anarchist movement. Today, anarchism largely consists of scattered handfuls of people operating on the fringe of the statist left opposition culture.

This is precisely the problem. Anarchists have yet to adapt themselves to the situation presented by the current world conditions and develop a comprehensive ideological framework through which the dominant political, economic and intellectual paradigms can be challenged. Typically, anarchists operate as if they were only another faction of the radical left, both politically and culturally. Today, "anarchism" is largely an amalgam of nostalgia for the classical movement (usually in the form of "revolutionary" groups that are by and large just history clubs), carry-over elements from the counter culture and New Left politics of the 1960s, the culture of "political correctness" developed by 1980s and 1990s liberals and social democrats, a type of Gandhi-wannabe "non-violence" rhetoric, the romanticizing of Third World revolutionary figures (including many decidedly non-anarchists), the punk rock subculture, an enthusiasm for critical theory and other hip intellectual trends and a general championing of every left-liberal popular cause yet to be invented.

The statist left is largely a discredited failure. Bourgeois social democracy has largely become the dominant ideology of the left wing of the ruling class and interest in Communist or other forms of far left opposition is largely non-existent outside of the world of academic neo-Marxists. Meanwhile, the resurgence of the libertarian right has become a powerful attraction for those looking for a movement to oppose the state. However penetrating the criticisms of the state advanced by the libertarian right may be, its decidedly bourgeois character ultimately prevents it from developing a comprehensive critique of class relations and the role of corporate power in maintaining modern systems of tyranny.

What is needed then is a new and improved form of anarchism that draws on the insights of the classical movement, corrects for its failings, expands its agenda and simultaneously utilizes the advances in historical study and economic science that have come about in recent decades. This would be an anarchism that rejects with equal fervor the statist left and corporate right and positions itself as diametrically opposed to the dominant "left-right" paradigm of contemporary political thought and discourse. This would involve a number of key changes in both contemporary anarchist ideology and strategy.

Introduction: Anarchism or Anarcho-Social Democracy

The first order of business for any form of serious anarchism must, of course, be opposition to the state itself. Many contemporary anarchists seem to have lost sight of this. Indeed, it is not uncommon for many of today's anarchists to take positions on the role of the state in society virtually indistinguishable from those of social democrats and even Communists. Even so perceptive an anarchist thinker as Noam Chomsky has fallen into this trap. The apparent enthusiasm of many so-called anarchists for the bourgeois "welfare state", for example, indicates that they have not developed any critique of the state beyond that advanced by ordinary leftwing theoreticians who see the state merely as an expression of the economic power of the capitalist class. This view ignores the classical Bakuninist position that the state is a social class in and of itself with power and privilege beyond that of even the economic elite. The only serious critics of this aspect of the state these days appear to be the "anarcho-capitalist" theoreticians who have developed a critique of the state and "big business" far more radical and penetrating than that offered by anyone on the contemporary left. That so many of the contemporary urban poor have been enslaved and made wards of the state by the welfare plantation operated by the social democratic left while anarchists look on with utter obliviousness is indeed tragic. This is an issue where anarchists should be taking the ideological lead but has instead been left to black conservatives, the corporate right and minority nationalists like the Nation of Islam.

It is necessary for anarchists to develop a consistent and principled opposition to the state in all its various aspects from the welfare system to "public" schools to the military-industrial complex to the repressive apparatus of so-called "criminal justice". The most centralized and powerful forms of the state must be the primary targets of the wrath of anarchists. This means that there must be a certain hierarchy of priorities for those with an anti-state agenda. Expressions of global statism must be the first enemy to be dealt with. The current process of "globalization" (conversion to rule by international conglomerates through international agencies) or the New World Order, as the populist right likes to call it, threatens to subjugate both the working classes and traditional nation-states and national cultures under the boot of a global corporate bureaucracy and monoculture. Therefore, all enemies of the globalization process become natural allies in the struggle. This would include nationalists, separatists, traditionalists and religious conservatives from the right and labor unions, environmentalists, socialists and Marxists and other radical "progressives" from the left.

The next order of business is to oppose the most powerful nation-states. Foremost among these would be the current ruling regime of the United States, the most powerful political and military empire in world history. All enemies of U.S. imperialism become allies on this point from the EZLN to the Shining Path to the Taliban to Fidel Castro. This does not mean that we embrace the politics or policies of any of these elements. It simply means that we work for the weakening of our greatest enemy first. The next group of nation-states to be opposed would be those most closely aligned with either globalization or U.S. imperialism. These include the nations of the NATO alliance, the Group of Seven and the racist, theocratic, Zionist regime imposed on Palestinian Arabs, Muslims, Jews and Christians alike by western imperial powers. Next on the international level, we oppose those states with the most widespread or grotesque abuses of "human rights"- Russia, China, Iran and Iraq, Cambodia, Indonesia and others. Lastly, we work for an end to states all together.

Within the domestic United States, we need to apply the same principles. That means that we oppose the federal government first, followed by state and local governments. Any devolution of power from the higher levels of government to the lower is to be supported. Any transfer of government functions from the state to non-government institutions is to be supported. All institutions, organizations and individuals operating in opposition to the state are to be supported whether they are tax resisters, homeschoolers, armed militias, street gangs, squatters, prisoners engaged in revolt, political protestors, and operators of pirate radio or whatever.

The most predatory aspects of the state should be the first to be opposed. Foremost among these are the police, prisons and so-called "criminal justice". Any measure reducing the number of laws, the powers of the police and courts and the ability of prison administrations to exercise arbitrary authority over inmates is to be supported. Those persons most persecuted by the state should be the first to be defended. In the current situation, this would mean prisoners, victims of drug war repression in all its forms, the homeless, youth, low-income workers, the urban poor, farmers run off their lands, street level entrepreneurs, prostitutes and other outcasts. I am always appalled when anarchists spend more time protesting against circuses and fast food restaurants than narcotics agents and vice cops, zoning inspectors, school authorities and the prison industry.

All control by the state over social life is to be resisted. This means that we should align ourselves with leftwing and rightwing anti-globalists, anti-militarists, anti-imperialists, separatists and secessionists. Along with the left, we should oppose police brutality, racism and sexism, the destruction of the environment, the death penalty, infringements on sexual freedom and abortion rights, the exploitation of workers and censorship. Along with the right, we should oppose state controlled schools, gun laws (unbelievably, many so-called anarchists have gone so far as to endorse control over firearms by the state), taxes, zoning laws that are largely a means of regulating the poor, the welfare system, repression against religious minorities, speech codes and other forms of leftwing censorship and restrictions on freedom of association.

These principles should be applied to the economic realm in a similar way. All state support for corporations should be opposed. Efforts to "democratize" or allow workers greater participation in industrial organizations is to be supported. The development of worker owned and operated enterprises should also be on the agenda along with opposition to harassment by government regulators of small enterprises and the self-employed. As government at various levels owns more than half of all the land in the U.S., a comprehensive land reform agenda is in order. Land reform should emphasize the rights of "use-possession", squatters, farmers and small entrepreneurs, families, cooperatives and individuals.

Strategically, we need to follow the example of the most successful anarchist forces of all time — the Spanish anarchist revolutionaries. Our revolutionary agenda should be to develop an alliance of community organizations, unions, cooperatives, enterprises, service organizations, youth clubs, study groups and other popular associations backed up by our guerrilla, paramilitary and militia forces armed for the purpose of seizing control on a city-by-city, county-by-county, state-by-state basis and the complete eradication of centralized state-corporate power and the elimination of the control of all our enemies. As America was the first classical liberal nation, it would indeed be an appropriate irony for it to be the first libertarian socialist nation as well.

Anarchism vs. Right-Wing Anti-Statism

Brian Oliver Sheppard's timely and poignant article "Anarchism vs. Right-Wing 'Anti-Statism" correctly points out the failure of the anarchist movement to provide an adequate response to and critique of the attacks on so-called "Big Government" that are so widespread in contemporary American political culture. Both Democrats and Republicans, liberals and conservatives, play at this game, hoping that the use of such rhetoric will serve to marshal popular frustration with ever-widening repression towards hypocritical and demagogic politicians promising to "end big government as we know it". Sheppard points out the sham behind such rhetoric eloquently. Now more than ever, anarchists need to develop a comprehensive and penetrating critique of the role of the state as a self-imposed monopoly of armed, coercive force that exists for the purpose of protecting and expanding class privilege and exploitation, war and imperialism, racism and tyranny.

Perhaps some of my own past experiences could be helpful here. About a decade ago, I was on a television talk show discussing anarchism with the show's host, a notorious liberal, and another guest, a Libertarian Party member. The more I attacked government, the more the host would reply, "God, you're starting to sound a lot like Ronald Reagan". I was left in the position of having to explain, through sound bite, the difference between the mercantilist, corporatist, fake "anti-statism" of the Republican-oriented Right and the genuinely liberatory class struggle traditions of classical anarchism. I am still having this debate with "conservative" minded relatives and associates who utterly fail to grasp the elitist, classist nature of the "antigovernment" rhetoric of mainstream political figures. I currently co-host a talk show on a public access cable channel and sometimes confused callers and letter writers will ask, "How can you be against government and corporations at the same time?" or "Don't you know that without government we would all be at the mercy of corporate predators?" Persons who think this way, whether from the left or the right, are showing that they have fallen victim to the false dichotomy between state and corporate power created by established state-capitalist ideology. If anarchists are going to win this debate, it is essential that we develop a system of analysis that consistently and effectively debunks the pseudo-analysis put forth by the apologists for the system.

The American political/economic system might be best described as "state-capitalism" (as Noam Chomsky calls it) or "corporate socialism" (a term Russell Means of AIM preferred to use). The primary purpose of the state is to maintain a monopoly of force over a particular geographical area, suppress internal dissent of any effectiveness and promote American imperial interests in other parts of the world. Economically, the U.S. system is a form of advanced mercantilism or, again quoting Chomsky, a "welfare state for the rich". Irrespective of rhetoric to the contrary, the U.S. elite class wants neither a genuine "free market" nor a genuine "socialism." Market discipline is to be used only to keep the "proles" in line. Subsidy and protection are the main orders of business for the state-corporate elite. On these points, I believe most anarchists would agree. Current "anti-state" rhetoric utilized by spokespersons for elite class interests represents a shift in elite class strategy for subjugation of the masses that has been taking place over the last quarter century. It is important that these matters be recognized and effectively addressed and, in the process, a number of flaws in contemporary anarchist thought and rhetoric might be detected. By "flaw", I am referring to the acquiescence of so many anarchists on the question of the so-called welfare state.

A dozen years ago, I would have argued that a welfare state and its various trappings (social security, "public" housing, "public" schools, state-paid medical care, "civil rights" legislation, etc.) were a necessary and vital part of the transitional phase between capitalism and a worker-controlled, socialized economy. I viewed "progressive" legislation and "big government programs" (as the right likes to call them) as forms of concession gained from elite class interests. I now believe that I was profoundly mistaken due to my own naiveté and ignorance of political and economic history. This is the position that many anarchists, including Chomsky, continue to maintain and Sheppard hints that this is his position as well. However, I feel that a position of this type is woefully inadequate in the formulation of a comprehensive anarchist critique of state and corporate power. Before I explain my position further, I want to digress a bit and mention what, I believe, has been a serious mistake that anarchists have made throughout much of our history. Our reliance on Marxist analysis for our understanding of political economy should be abandoned.

For Marxists, the state is simply an expression of capitalist class power. The state is the capitalists' political arm, its "executive committee", as I think old Karl once described it. The solution to the problem of class exploitation is for the workers and their allies to simply seize control of the state and convert it into an instrument of working class power, a "workers' state". However, this position, as anarchists from Bakunin onward pointed out, ignores the essentially coercive and authoritarian nature of the state, whether feudal, capitalist, socialist or whatever. As anarchists, we oppose not just capitalist power and authority but power and authority of any kind. This fatal error in the realm of class analysis employed by many anarchists (including myself at one point) has brought us to the point where, I believe, we have often ended up taking contradictory and, to an outside observer, seemingly absurd positions on the role of state intervention in the economy. It is not enough for anarchists to take positions on economics virtually indistinguishable from those of liberals or even Communists (our historical archenemies). A better approach is needed.

The purpose of the welfare states, maintained by state-capitalist regimes, is not to assist the workers and the poor but to co-opt, subjugate, weaken and control them. Historically, as modern welfare states have expanded, genuinely revolutionary workers movements have declined. Ideologically, the earliest proponents of the welfare state were elite class intellectuals such as the utilitarians Jeremy Bentham and John Stuart Mill. These and others like them viewed welfare states as a means of controlling and pacifying the unruly masses. The first modern welfare state was the military dictatorship of Otto von Bismarck, who implemented a social security system as a means of inculcating allegiance to and piety towards the state among the general population. The American version of the welfare state (admittedly pale by world standards) began as a response to the labor upheavals of the twenties and thirties. What purposes of population control do the various features of the welfare state serve?

State-assistance programs condition the people to regard the state as a benefactor, a type of bureaucratic "sugar daddy," rather than as an instrument of their own exploitation and repression. I once had an elderly relative ask me, "Why would you want to overthrow the government when they do so much good for us like social security, school lunch programs, student loans…." and on and on. The welfare state is used by the elite class to create dependency by the masses on themselves thereby weakening their spirit of resistance. Those who feed you can control you. Of course, this does not mean that we adopt the standard right-wing line of blaming the poor for their own exploitation at the hands of the welfare state created by the elite class. Rather, it means that we work for the empowerment of the people rather than the bureaucracy. What should the stance of the anarchists in regards to the welfare state be?

For starters, we should follow the advice of the late Sam Dolgoff who maintained that workers should demand their entire pay without deductions of any kind (income taxes, social security, corporate insurance programs) and instead create our own health care, old age, disability, etc. programs under our control through our own mutual aid and solidarity organizations (unions, cooperatives, clubs, community groups). We need to organize claimants' unions for the recipients of "public" assistance and demand direct cash payments to the beneficiaries themselves rather than vouchers, coupons and stamps issued by government agencies. "Public" schools, institutions created for the purpose of indoctrinating children with elite class ideology, should be scrapped in favor of progressive educational services established by our own working class oriented revolutionary organizations (perhaps modeled after Summerhill or the Modern School). Workers organizations should demand the expulsion of both corporate overseers and government sponsored "regulatory" bureaucrats from our workplaces in favor of direct self-management and self-regulation by the workers themselves. "Public" housing authorities should be scrapped, their offices destroyed, and tenants should assume direct management of their own housing facilities. These same principles would, of course, apply to tenants renting from "private" landlords, the self-employed and farmers dealing with state-supervisory agencies, consumers' interests and so on. The final aim, of course, should be the dismantling of the false dichotomy between the "public" and "private" sectors and the socialization and communalization of state and corporate resources under the direct control of our worker, consumer, tenant and community organizations.

As I mentioned, current "antigovernment" rhetoric employed by elite class mouthpieces represents, I believe, a certain laziness and complacency that the "powers that be" have sunken into. So successful have their efforts of the past thirty years to co-opt and subjugate the people through social democratic welfare state policies that they no longer think it is worth the bother. They no longer see the need to even put on the charade of maternalistic government, which they view as costly and not generating enough profits for corporate interests in the same way that the rapidly expanding prison-industrial complex and other recently emergent forms of repression are doing. Consequently, we see renewed attacks on our class in every area. Gentrification and "urban revitalization" are displacing the traditional urban poor. "Welfare reform" is displacing those enslaved to the state via "public assistance." Nearly ten million people have been dispossessed of their traditional lands across the farm belt of the American heartland. Three million people, perhaps more, are living in the street and repression against the homeless is rising. One in thirty people, perhaps more, are in the direct clutches of the state by means of the prison-industrial complex and the repressive apparatus of so-called "criminal justice". The availability, affordability and quality of health care have declined due the centralization of health care services under oligopolistic HMO's. Now that U.S. warmongering and imperialism can no longer be justified with shallow Cold War rhetoric, the American regime simply undertakes violent assaults on other societies on whatever whim it fancies at the moment or for no apparent reason at all. The elite class is creating a powder keg that will eventually erupt in a rather big way.

Although I agree with Sheppard's analysis of elite class "antigovernment" propaganda, I disagree with his apparent failure to distinguish between the corporatist, mercantilist, semi fascist Republican oriented right-wing on one hand and the more populist, decentralist, libertarian right on the other. To illustrate this distinction I would refer to a statement issued by Ted Kaczynski regarding his conversations with Tim McVeigh at the federal prison where they were both being held:

> McVeigh told me of his idea (which I think may have significant merit) that certain rebellious elements on the American right and left respectively had more in common with one another than is commonly realized, and that the two groups ought to join forces. This led us to discuss, though only briefly, the question of what constitutes the 'right'. I pointed out that the word 'right', in the political sense, was originally associated with authoritarianism,

and I raised the question of why certain radically anti-authoritarian groups (such as the Montana Freemen) were lumped together with authoritarian factions as the 'right'. McVeigh explained that the American far right could be roughly divided into two branches, the fascist/racist branch, and the individualistic or "freedom-loving" branch which generally was not racist. (Ted Kaczynski, quoted in American Terrorist, by Lou Michel and Dan Herbeck)

When two individuals who, as much as anyone else, have given their lives and freedom to take up arms against the system, suggest a libertarian-left / libertarian-right collaboration, perhaps we should give them ear.[1] I have had rather extensive contact with the militia/patriot movement and other similar elements, so perhaps I could shed some light on these matters for anarchists. The overwhelming majority of militia members and right-libertarian populists are not racists. The racist element in the militia movement is largely confined to small groups, usually consisting of four or five people, who comprise, at best, ten percent of the movement and are steadily disavowed by other militia groups. Most organized hate groups specifically oppose the militias because they are antigovernment rather than anti-Jewish or anti-African. Militias have essentially the same enemies that we do-government, corporations, banks, cops, prisons, schools, the corporate media, the military-industrial complex, etc. The difference is primarily cultural. Anarchists stand for the liberation of all the oppressed regardless of national or cultural identity. Militia/patriot people view themselves as standing for "American values" which they regard as the Jeffersonian/classical liberal idea of "life, liberty and the pursuit of happiness" and all that. Now, this might seem quaint and childish to us but it is hardly ominous. Many of these people are also strong cultural conservatives and, predictably, have less than

---

1   Although I am pro-armed struggle, I disagree with the specific actions taken by both McVeigh and Kaczynski. McVeigh killed people who had absolutely nothing to do with any of the issues including office workers, janitors, truck drivers and children. Kaczynski's targets were mostly small fish only peripherally connected to the problems he perceived.

enlightened views on feminism, gay/lesbian issues, religion, et.al but no more so than many ordinary Palestinians, Iraqis or, for that matter, American trade unionists, many African-American and Hispanic-American working class males, many prisoners, traditional Catholic Latin American peasants and plenty of others whose struggles we would otherwise support. I've seen more than a few militia people reading Noam Chomsky, Michael Parenti, William Blum and other similar writers. Most patriot groups I have encountered generally favor a decentralized society, extensive individual freedom, abolition of state-run militaries in favor of a volunteer civilian militia, a common law legal system based on negotiation between contending parties, and other similar ideas that are not quite so far removed from those of many anarchists. They typically oppose the drug war, the prison industry, U.S. imperialism and the corporate-state. I have seen militia publications criticizing the police attack on the MOVE group in Philadelphia in 1985. There is an all-African militia in Detroit and similar groups in other cities. Many militia people express sympathy for the EZLN, IRA, PLO, the Black Panthers and AIM. We do ourselves a disservice by dismissing these people so cavalierly. We need to expand our outreach efforts and find new allies whenever and wherever we can whether they are left-wing, right-wing or no wing at all.

Shachtman, Marcuse and Bakunin

It is a great irony that the two principal factions of the present day American ruling class, the Republicans and Democrats, are currently under the intellectual leadership of ideological tendencies derived from neo-Marxism. The neoconservatives who currently lead the Republican Party and therefore the present administration are only a few decades removed from the right-wing Trotskyism of Max Shachtman. The career of Irving Kristol, who made the journey from orthodox Trotskyism in his youth to Shachtmanism to becoming the godfather of neo-conservatism, illustrates and personifies this evolutionary process perfectly. Likewise, the abandonment of its traditional working class constituency by the Democratic Party in favor of identity politics, victimology and cultural leftism illustrates the coming to power of the New Left of the 1960s, whose intellectual guru Herbert Marcuse sought to revise Marxism by transferring the basis of the class struggle from labor within the context of political economy to officially designated victim groups within the context of cultural criticism.

That both neo-conservatism and cultural Marxism in practice closely resemble traditional fascism should come as no surprise given that most of the founding fathers of classical fascism were former Marxists. Indeed, it has long been recognized by astute observers that Marxism in power bears striking similarities to fascism or "national socialism." Even the New Left icon Susan Sontag once referred to Soviet Marxism as "red fascism". Throughout the twentieth century, a variety of thinkers, so-called "elite theorists" or "new class theorists" or "neo-Machiavellians", argued that the contending systems of Soviet Marxism, German or Italian fascism and American or British corporate-welfarism were really just variations of the same basic system, what James Burnham called "managerialism." That the formerly Trotskyite neoconservatives should incorporate Straussian fascism into their ideological framework should come as no surprise to anyone familiar with Mussolini's abandonment of Marxism in favor of proponents of the "conservative revolution". That a Democratic administration led by former New Leftists like the Clintons should adopted overtly fascistic tendencies (such as Mrs. Clinton's plans for reorganizing the US health care industry on the model of Mussolini's corporatism, police state-oriented "anti-terrorism" legislation and the overt police state massacre at Waco) should come as no surprise to anyone familiar with the careers of Juan and Eva Peron, who camouflaged their fascistic tendencies under the veneer of a leftist-populist cover ideology.

The prediction made a century ago by the classical liberal economist William Graham Sumner that men would one day be divided into only two political camps, Socialists and Anarchists, is now on the verge of realization. Marxism and its derivatives, principally neo-conservatism and cultural Marxism, are now the dominant ideological perspectives in all of the modern countries. The early anarchist thinker and rival of Marx, Mikhail Bakunin, noted that if state-socialism ever came to power, it would produce the bloodiest tyrannies in history, which it eventually did in the forms of the "managerial" states of the last century. But now things are coming full circle. Gabriel Kolkhoz recently noted that, since the disappearance of the Soviet Union as a restraining force, global resistance to American hegemony has become more and more widespread, more effective and more decentralized in the form of what William Lind calls "fourth generation warfare", the essence of which pits conventional states against non-state entities. Along the same lines, Martin Van Creveld predicts that the era of large national states of the type traditionally glorified by Jacobins and Marxists is on its way out, with decentralized, heterogeneous, smaller scale polities being the wave of the future. Indeed, it might be argued that the overthrow of the New World Order and the nation-state system by the fourth generation forces signifies the ultimate and perfect vengeance against the Marxists by the Anarchists for the events of the First International, Kronstadt and Barcelona. Could it be that the Marxists did indeed conquer the "world to be won" only to have it pulled out from underneath them by their pesky Anarchist enemies who, as Rothbard noted, "shall repeal the twentieth century"?

The Fruits of Anarchist "Anti-Racism"

"Certain attitudes derived from the New Left and the so-called counter-culture permeated neo-anarchism and had a deleterious effect upon it. Chief among these was elitism. It was the common belief among the New Left that the majority of the population was "co-opted", "sold-out", "racist" and "sexist". For the hippie-left, most people were considered to be beer-swilling, short-haired rednecks. Much of this youthful hostility was directed against their parents and hence was more of an expression of adolescent rebellion than political insight. With the exception of those who opted for anarcho-syndicalism, most neo-anarchists carried this contemptuous attitude with them. The majority was written-off as hopelessly corrupted and this attitude still continues today. Such contempt is in complete contrast to classical anarchism, which even at its most vanguardist, saw itself as only a catalyst or spokesman for the masses. While rejecting the majority, they became infatuated with minorities. The New Left, scorning workers, turned to racial minorities and the "poor" as possible agents of social change. Native people, prisoners, drop-outs, homosexuals, all have been given a high profile, virtually to the exclusion of the rest of the population."

-Larry Gambone, *Sane Anarchy*, 1995

An article in the *Intelligence Report*, the journal of the state-connected, crony-capitalist, cop-friendly, "private" espionage and surveillance agency known the Southern Poverty Law Center remarked: *"Unifying anarchists has been likened to herding cats. But if there is one theme that most anarchists will rally around, it is that of stamping out racism, especially organized racism driven by white nationalist ideology. Many younger anarchists are members of Anti-Racist Action, a national coalition of direct-action "antifa" (short for "anti-fascist") groups that confront neo-Nazis and racist skinheads in the street, often resulting in violence."*

And what do these anarchists have to show for all of this "anti-racist" zealotry? How well are these anarchists regarded by actually existing people of color for their efforts? An item that has recently been circulating in the anarchist milieu with the revealing title, "Smack a White Boy, Round Two", demonstrates just how much "solidarity" is felt towards the mostly, white, middle-class, left-anarchist movement by the supposed beneficiaries of its anti-racism:

> *Dread locked white punks, crusties with their scabies friends, and travelling college bros swarmed a space on the dividing line of gentrification in the Bloomfield/Garfield/Friendship area late July 2009 in Pittsburgh for the annual CrimethInc convergence. Whereas previous CrimethInc convergences had been located deep in wooded areas, this particular one took place in a poor, black neighborhood that is being pushed to the borders by entering white progressive forces.*

> *There were those that had experienced CrimethInc's oppressive culture and people for years and others who had experienced enough oppression after just a few days. Our goals were to stop CrimethInc, their gentrifying force, and to end the convergence right then and there for all that they had done.*

> *Just a few blocks away, eight anarchist/autonomous/anti-authoritarian people of color* gathered to discuss a direct confrontation. We arrived from different parts of these stolen lands of the Turtle Island. Some came from the Midwest, some from the Northeast, some born and raised in Pittsburgh. Altogether we represented 7 different locations, half of us socialized as female a variety of sizes, skin color, with identities of queers, trans, gender-queers, gender variants, and womyn. With little time and a desire for full consensus, we quickly devised a plan.*

The majority of the CrimethInc kids were in the ballroom on the second floor watching and participating in a cabaret. A group of us began gathering attendees' packs, bags, shoes, banjos, and such from the other rooms on the second floor and moving it all down the hallway towards the stairs. We had gone pretty unnoticed, mostly due to lack of lighting.

Once those rooms had been emptied, it was time for the main event. We gathered at the ballroom's doorway furthest from the stairs following the final act of the cabaret.

"On the count of three. One, two, three!" one APOCista said.

"Get the fuck out!", we all shouted.

And the eviction began. One apocer began reading 'An Open Letter to White Radicals/Progressives', while the others began yelling at the attendees to gather their things and leave. Irritated by their continued inaction after about 10 minutes or so, one of the people involved in the action shouted,

"This is not an act! Get your shit, or we'll remove it for you!"

So much for anarchists as the exemplars of multicultural brotherly love. Now, before I get to other questions, let me say that I actually think the "Anarchist People of Color" group who carried out this "eviction" had a point. Many white leftists and progressives do indeed regard non-whites as children in need of rescue by enlightened folks such as themselves, and often assume a paternalistic attitude when dealing with people of color. And while I'm not so sure that "gentrification" by white anarchist kids is quite on the level of gentrification by upper-middle class, affluent, professional people organized into state-connected "civic organizations" and "business associations", and operating in collusion with crony-capitalist "developers", the overall point is still well-taken. Gentrification does indeed frequently assume the character of a kind of urban imperialism, and white, middle-class "progressives" who never tire of wearing their racial liberalism on their sleeves are often at the forefront of such efforts. Indeed, it might be argued that gentrification serves the same purpose in modern urban societies as the dispossession of native or indigenous peoples' in frontier or colonial societies, i.e., naked robbery carried out under the banner of enlightenment, progress, and paternalism or cultural and class chauvinism. Some would go even further and argue that mass immigration serves a similar purpose, e.g., economic and cultural dispossession of the indigenous poor and working class in order to provide labor for capitalists, clients for social services bureaucrats and voters for political parties and ethnic lobbies. But that might be "racism".

The obsession with "racism" exhibited by modern leftists appears to be rooted in a number of things. Some are the obvious, e.g., the political, cultural and intellectual backlash against such horrors as Nazism, South African apartheid, "Jim Crow" in the American South, the Vietnam War and other manifestations of extreme colonialism. Another is the need for the radical Left to find a new cause once the horrors of Communism were revealed. Still another is the universalist ethos that emerged from Enlightenment rationalism. Yet another is the adolescent rebellion against society mentioned by Gambone. And another is the quasi-Christian moralism exhibited by many left-wingers: "Love thy exotically colored neighbor."

It's like this, my fellow anarchist comrades: World War Two is over. Hitler is dead. George Wallace is dead. Bull Conner is dead. Jim Crow has been relegated into the dustbin of history. Apartheid is finished, and Nelson Mandela eventually became South Africa's head of state. In case you haven't been paying attention, the United States now has a black President. Many of the largest American cities have black-dominated governments. In the wider society, "racism" has become the ultimate sin, much like communism or homosexuality might have been in the 1950s. By continuing to beat the dead horse of "white supremacy", anarchists are simply making our movement look like fools.

No doubt there are many reading this that will raise the issues of the high rates of imprisonment among blacks and Hispanics, police brutality, the medical neglect of illegal immigrants in detention centers, or the high unemployment rates in American inner cities. Do you really think that no whites have ever been adversely affected by these things? Do you think there are no whites in jail or prison for frivolous reasons? Who receive shoddy medical care? Who are adversely affected by state-capitalism and plutocratic rule? Who are subject to police harassment or violence, or who are shabbily treated by agents or bureaucrats of the state? Who are subject to social ostracism because of their class, culture, religion or lifestyle?

There is certainly nothing wrong with opposing the genuine oppression of people of other races or colors, and many anarchists and other radicals engage in laudable displays of support for the people of Palestine, Iraq, Afghanistan, Tibet, Latin America, and indigenous ethnic groups who are subjected to occupation or imperialist aggression. Yet, the obsession with "racism" found among many Western radicals has become pathological in nature. Whenever I encounter these "anti-racism" hysterics, I am reminded of the cultic, fundamentalist religious sects, where no amount of devotion to the cause is ever good enough. Go to church three times a week? Not good enough, you need to be there six times a week. And there is little doubt that the war between Anarchist People of Color and Crimethinc will produce a great deal of "What are we doing wrong, us shitty white supremacists?" self-flagellation among many "anti-racist" left-anarchists.

This obsession with "racism" on the part of many anarchists might be worth it if it had the effect of recruiting or converting many thousands or millions of people of color to our cause. Yet, the simple truth is that decades of anti-racism hysteria has produced an anarchist movement that is as white as it ever was. This does not mean that there are never any non-whites to be found in anarchist circles. Of course there are. But are they representative of the cultural norms of the ethnic or racial groups from where they came? Not in my experience. Instead, the relatively small numbers of people of color who can be found in North American anarchist circles are usually immigrants from other places, or products of ethnic minority cultures that have assimilated into a wider white culture, for instance, blacks who grew up in white middle-class neighborhoods or minorities who participate in white youth subcultures, like punk rock. Honestly speaking, what would a typical African-American or Latino think if they wandered into the standard anarchist discussion group and found themselves in the midst of the usual anarchist banter about "racism"? What would they think, other than, "What a bunch of freaks!"

This does not mean that anarchists should become "pro-racist". It simply means that it would be more productive if anarchists would simply re-orient themselves towards the ostensible purpose of anarchism, i.e., *"a political philosophy encompassing theories and attitudes which consider the state, as compulsory government, to be unnecessary, harmful, and/or undesirable, and promote the elimination of the state or anarchy."* I recently came across a Facebook page with the heading "The Other Anarchists" which described itself thus: *"For those who wish to see the state abolished, but are not nihilists, terrorists, or idiots. Including some: free market anti-capitalists, anarcho-capitalists, anarcho-monarchists, voluntaryists, social anarchists, Christian anarchists, Green anarchists, and our fellow-travelers ([non-violent] Luddites, paleoconservatives, minarchists, left-conservatives, retroprogressives, and the like)."*

This would seem to be about right. Perhaps we can work with the nihilists and terrorists, but the idiots really need to be shown the door. What should anarchists do about "racism"? *Just forget about it.* Yes, you read that right. Many anarchists engage in many worthwhile projects that many different kinds of people can benefit from, like antiwar activism, labor solidarity, prisoner defense, support for the homeless, and resistance to police brutality, the protection of animals from cruelty, environmental preservation, alternative media or alternative education. These are issues that transcend color lines. Just stick to these and let "people of color" work out their own problems for themselves.

The APOC/Crimethinc battle may well be indicative of what the future of the political Left will be. I have predicted before that the center-left will be dominant in American politics for the next several decades due to demographic, cultural and generational change in U.S. society. It is widely predicted that the non-white populations will collectively outnumber whites in the U.S. by the 2040s. As the non-white population grows due to demographic trends and large-scale immigration, and as class divisions widen, there is likely to be a split within liberalism between the mostly white, upper middle class, cultural progressives and the mostly black and Hispanic lower classes, which include many persons with more conservative views on social questions like gender roles, abortion, homosexuality and religion.

A Zogby poll concerning the level of public sympathy for the matter of secession indicated that the principal source of support for genuinely radical ideas (like separatism) comes not from the "far right" or backwoods militiamen but from young, unemployed, uneducated blacks and Hispanics in the heavily populated areas of the U.S.. In a few decades, the crumbling U.S. Empire and its liberal-capitalist-multiculturalist elites and affluent classes may well be facing an insurgency by the expanded non-white underclass. There are an estimated one million urban gang members in the U.S., mostly blacks and Hispanics, and these are organized into thousands of armed groups. Are these not a domestic American version of the "fourth generation" insurgent movements that exist in other parts of the world like Latin America or the Middle East?

What will be the condition of American society in the decades ahead as the liberal-capitalist-multiculturalist ruling class begins to lose its grip and is faced with an insurgency by the black and Hispanic underclass? What should be the response of the mostly white anarchist movement to such a turn of events? How should the anarchist movement seek to handle such a scenario? Play your cards wrong and you'll end up in a situation infinitely worse than that faced by Crimethinc.

The Fruits of Anarchist "Anti-Racism"

The anarchist milieu needs to re-think its positions concerning racial matters. Continuing to perpetrate anti-racism hysteria year after year, decade after decade, is a dead end. There is zero evidence that such a stance will bring the masses of North American blacks and Hispanics into our ranks, and much compelling evidence that such efforts are futile, foolish and counterproductive. For many years, the anarchist movement's obsession with "social issues" has been a distraction from what ought to be the primary objective of anarchism, i.e., the abolition of the state. This is not to say that anti-statism is the only value, or that anarchists should not be concerned with other matters. It does mean that a more constructive stance on certain questions should be pursued.

For one thing, it might be helpful if anarchists would display an interest in issues other than run of the mill left-wing causes like those involving race, gender, sexual orientation, ecology and the like. Why are anarchists not involved in the movement for the defense of the right to keep and bear arms? In a sensible anarchist movement, there would be anarchists sitting on the board of directors of the National Rifle Association. Why are anarchists not involved in the various movements for local or regional autonomy, or secession by states and communities? Certainly, such efforts should fit well with the supposed anarchist emphasis on decentralization.

What might be a more sensible approach to racial and cultural differences than the hysterical approach currently taken? A venerable American tradition is one of "separation of church and state." This is a tradition that has worked quite well throughout U.S. history. Individual Americans are largely free to practice or not practice whatever religion they wish. Yes, fringe religious groups like the Branch Davidians are sometimes subject to persecution. Yes, state laws such as the ban on the use of psychedelic drugs impedes powerless groups like certain indigenous tribes from practicing their religion. Yes, children from sects whose tenants prohibit certain medical practices are sometimes forcibly subjected to such practices. Yes, religious do-gooders sometimes wish to use the force of the laws to suppress activities deemed immoral, like gambling, vice or alcohol. But for the most part, most people practice their religion or non-religion of choice most of the time with very little interference from either the state, or from society at-large. Compare this with the situation in, say, Saudi Arabia or North Korea, and it can be determined that "separation of church and state" is a system that works quite well. Research shows, for instance, that atheists are a minority group that is more widely disliked than any of the groups championed by the Left: blacks, immigrants, homosexuals, Muslims. Yet atheists, of whom I am one, are hardly an "oppressed minority" but an intellectually and culturally elite group who are heavily represented within the ranks of leading scientists, philosophers, academics, journalists, authors, artists and entertainers. As far back as 1910, Thomas Edison was able to proclaim his heretical religious views with to the *New York Times* with impunity.

I submit that the appropriate attitude for anarchists to take concerning racial and cultural matters is one of "separation of race and state" or "separation of culture and state." Within such a context, all state legislation or regulation concerning race and culture would be eliminated, and individuals and groups would be able to engage in whatever racial or cultural practices they wished within the context of their own voluntary associations. Just as some religious organizations or institutions are very conservative or exclusionary in nature, and others are very liberal and inclusive, so might some racial or cultural organizations and institutions be similarly conservative or liberal, exclusionary or inclusive. For instance, the Anarchist People of Color and other like-minded groups could have their own schools, communities, neighborhoods, commercial enterprises and other institutions where white folks are verboten. Likewise, the Nation of Islam, Aztlan Nation, evangelical Christians, Mormons, Paleoconservatives, or "national-anarchists" might also have their own homogenous communities as well. Feminists and queers might implement similar arrangements for themselves.

The Fruits of Anarchist "Anti-Racism"

As I have said before, we need a "revolution within anarchism itself." We need an anarchist movement that is not just an all-purposes leftist movement, but a movement that has abolition of the state as its central focus, and an approach to matters of race, culture, religion and so forth that is workable in a highly diverse society. This renovated anarchist movement would shift its focus towards the building of autonomous, voluntary communities, reflecting a wide assortment of cultural, economic or ideological themes, within the context of a wider pan-separatist ethos whose principle enemy is the overarching state. It should be understood that severe and irreconcilable differences among different kinds of people will inevitably arise, and that such differences are best managed according to the principle of "peace through separatism." As Erik von Kuehnelt-Leddihn observed: "The ideological and philosophical struggles, which can neither be suppressed nor made an organic part of the governmental machine, have to be relegated to the private sphere of society."

Race, Culture and Immigration

Whenever I write on the subject of race, I always feel compelled to include evidence of my own anti-racist credentials. Race is a subject where frank but civil discussion is all but impossible in contemporary society. I am always amused by the "hate" mail that I get from knee-jerk racist fanatics and knee-jerk anti-racist fanatics alike. One group calls me "nigger lover" while the other labels me a "fascist". These juvenile slurs reflect the simple-mindedness of those who hurl them rather than any sort of accurate perception of my actual views.

My earliest political activism involved opposition to South African apartheid and the American war against the civilian populations of the Central American nations in the 1980s. I opposed apartheid because, then as now, I viewed it as an arrangement where one particular ethnic group was using its control over the state to suppress others, much like the current situation in contemporary Palestine. The apartheid regimes headed by P.W. Botha and F.W. De Klerk were de facto American puppets that served as outposts for U.S. ruling class interests on the African continent. The apartheid government was also pro-Zionist and sought to become nuclear armed with the help of Israel. Like my then-comrades on the American left, I believed the white South African regime had to go. Unlike my then-comrades, I always opposed the coming to power of the African National Congress and the South African Communist Party. Throughout those years, I would warn my cohorts on the left that these elements would simply replace a tyrannical white fascist government with a tyrannical black communist one a la Rhodesia/Zimbabwe. I gave my own support to the Congress of South African Trade Unions (COSATU), a mixed race, anti-communist, and anti-statist labor federation organized on the old anarcho-syndicalist model. I favored the political solution of Leon Leouw and Frances Kendall, a black and white South African respectively, who won a Nobel Prize for their book "After Apartheid." Their proposal involved the creation of a neutral South Africa that would be aligned with neither the United States nor the Soviet Union. A Swiss-style canton system would be established with there being some black cantons, some white cantons, cantons for other ethnic groups and racially mixed cantons. Different cantons could have different forms of government, from communism to free market liberalism. Unfortunately, it was not to be.

I took similar positions regarding Central America. I favored victory for the FMLN guerrillas of El Salvador not because I was thrilled with their politics, but because they were the only available alternative to the U.S.-backed terrorist regime, which received $1.5 million dollars in American aid daily, and practiced Pol Pot-style genocide against the rural population of the country. In Nicaragua, I supported the Sandinista regime against the CIA-created National Democratic Front, a terrorist group of former Somocistas who regularly massacred entire villages as part of their destabilization campaign. However, I also supported anti-Sandinista resistance forces. These included Miskito Indians who had suffered land confiscation and massacres at the hands of the Sandinista army, black Protestants in the western region seeking autonomy from the Hispanic Catholic dominated government in Managua, peasants forced to work on state-owned collective farms seeking land of their own and dissident Sandinistas like Eden Pastora who opposed the monopoly on power of the nine-man junta who controlled the Ortega regime.

I relate all of this obscure and seemingly irrelevant history to illustrate something I began to learn about the orthodox left during that time. My views in those days originated from my desire to see liberty triumph in those troubled nations. However, I soon realized that most of my leftist cohorts were interested not in the victory of liberty but in the victory of Communism and anti-white racism. Unfortunately, this was as true of the so-called "anarchist" factions of the left as it was of the more explicitly Marxist left. Hysterical "antiracism", mirroring the hysterical "anticommunism" of the traditional right, has become the foremost article of faith of the leftist-anarchist movement. Clearly, a more nuanced approach is sorely needed. Race relations in the United States are rapidly deteriorating. Historical evidence indicates that the eventual fate of multiethnic empires, of which the United States is one, is typically quite unpleasant. Informed and insightful commentators, such as Thomas Chittum,[1] have pointed out similarities between the circumstances that led to brutal ethnic wars in the former Yugoslavia and Central Africa and the current state of race relations in America. Thus far, the anarchist movement has failed miserably as far as the need to develop a cogent and coherent analysis of the racial situation in this country is concerned. Simply repeating archaic Leninist rhetoric about white supremacist conspiracies will not do.

The central issue in developing a solid anarchist position on racial questions involves the matter of the relationship between race and state. To examine this matter thoroughly, we have to go back to the beginnings of the American nation. Most historians do not recognize that there were essentially two American Revolutions in the late eighteenth century. Anarchists are typically aware of the two revolutions that occurred in Russian in 1917. The first, the March Revolution, brought the republic of Alexander Kerensky to power. The second, the October Revolution, brought the Communist regime of V.I. Lenin to power after a military coup initiated by the Bolshevik Party and its henchmen in the Red Army deposed the Kerensky government. Similarly, the American Revolution of 1776 involved a populist revolt against the British colonial governments in the thirteen original American states. The result was the Articles of Confederation, a highly decentralized, largely libertarian regime whose central body lacked the power of taxation. Pro-worker and pro-farmer governments were often elected at the state level. It has been said, for example,

1   "*Civil War Two*", by Thomas Chittum

that the Articles-era government of Pennsylvania was as close to a "dictatorship of the proletariat" as has ever existed in America.

The Articles of Confederation government was destroyed when the centralized federal regime was created by Alexander Hamilton and his cronies. The Hamiltonians represented northeastern mercantile, shipping and banking interests who desired a state-capitalist central government with which to advance their own economic interests. The powers delegated to the new federal government included the creation of a central navy to protect commercial vessels from pirate ships, subsidies to infrastructure, a central state monopoly on the issuance of currency to constrict the supply of capital, uniform bankruptcy laws to be imposed upon the states (state bankruptcy laws were regarded as too favorable to debtors), the creation of a large state-mandated "free trade area" for commercial interests, tariffs for the furtherance of mercantilist ambitions, monopoly privileges imposed by a patent system and other features of a mercantilist, state-capitalist infrastructure.[2] In its very essence, the federal government of the United States was established to be a state-capitalist class dictatorship from the very beginning.

The opponents of the creation of the federal government, the so-called "anti-federalists," included some of the most prominent, and most radical, early American revolutionaries such as Patrick Henry and Thomas Jefferson. Henry refused to serve in the US Senate out of his objection to the federal regime. Jefferson, in particular, was harshly anti-federalist and offered a radical decentralist alternative to both the federal regime and the state governments alike. He proposed "dividing the counties into wards" in the several states under a system of populist community self-management with a meritocratic, natural aristocracy of philosophers, intellectuals and scientists serving as societal leaders. Jefferson also opposed central banking and warned of the potential dangers posed by the then-nascent industrial capitalist

2   *Capitalism versus Free Enterprise* by Keith Preston

class. He favored the elimination of slavery and the creation of sovereign states for freed slaves in the territories west of the thirteen colonies. Jefferson also opposed a standing military and seriously downsized the US military forces during his term as president. He seems to have retained his radical decentralist views even during his term as President, which he accepted only to prevent the arch-reactionary Hamilton from achieving the position. Jefferson was about as close to an anarchist as existed among the intellectual classes in those days.

To understand the implications of all of this for contemporary racial issues, we can imagine how American society would have evolved if Jefferson's views had prevailed in his day. If slavery had been abolished, along with the British colonial occupation, and if blacks given their own land and a chance for free development, race relations would obviously have begun on a much more equitable footing in this country. If the federal government had not been created in the first place, there would have been no centralized state for northern capitalist interests to obtain control over and impose tyrannical tariffs and economic discrimination on the agricultural southern states. Without slavery and the Tariff of Abominations, there would have been no Civil War with its 625,000 casualties and the subsequent consolidation of a nationalist regime and the elimination of states' sovereignty. Even if slavery had not been abolished following the 1776 revolution, without a federal government there would have been no Fugitive Slave Laws and abolitionist sympathizers in the north would have been able to harbor escaped slaves if they desired.[3] Enclaves for liberated slaves could have been formed in the regions bordering the slave states and in sparsely populated areas of the south. These might have been used as launching points for guerrilla efforts against the slavocracy. In fact, the early American anarchist Lysander Spooner once drew up a plan of precisely this type.[4]

---

3   In the pre-Civil War era, some northern states threatened to secede from the federal union in protest of fugitive slave laws.

4   Lysander Spooner is much underappreciated in contemporary anarchist circles. His *No*

Without the federal government, there would have been no American invasion of the 1850s and seizure of a third of the Mexican nation. There would have been no land-grabbing of Indian territory. Western migration would have taken place anyway but it would have been slower and done on more equitable terms with the Indian nations. Skirmishes between whites and Indians still would have occurred but these would have been localized conflicts, akin to the inner-city gang wars of today. The unconstitutional annexation of the sovereign Republic of Texas by the United States would not have taken place. The absence of a centralized state would have rendered the centralization of wealth that led to the monopoly capitalism of the robber baron-era impossible. America would have remained a nation of small producers in a decentralized economy. Without the rise of the nationalist, mercantilist state and monopoly capitalism, there would have been no abandonment of traditional American neutrality ("isolationism") for the sake of capitalist interests in the Spanish-American War. There would have been no American entry into World War One, and therefore no destruction of imperial Germany, no Treaty of Versailles, no Hitler, no World War Two, no Soviet occupation of Eastern Europe, no destruction of continental Europe and Japan, no Cold War, no arms race, no American hegemony, no Korea or Vietnam, no military-industrial complex, no New World Order.

If our ancestors had applied their revolutionary ideals more consistently, America would today be a decentralized federation of sovereign territories and communities with a worker-farmer-inventor-artisan-merchant dominated economy with localized production for local use. We would have a Swiss-style neutralist foreign policy and a local militia-based defense force. The eastern and northern regions of the country would be predominately white, with moderate assimilation by other ethnic groups, bordered by prosperous southern and mid-western enclaves

---

Treason: The Constitution of No Authority, a refutation of the social contract theory behind the US Constitution, is a masterpiece. In the US Civil War, Spooner favored secession by the Confederacy and slave insurrections simultaneously.

and territories dominated primarily by blacks with largely harmonious trade and cultural relations taking place between the races. The southwest would be Mexican territory, highly prosperous because of its mineral wealth, with a large population of whites who serve as the region's primary technical workers. Texas would be a sovereign nation and an important trading partner. The west and northwest would be inhabited by a large Indian population mixed with a large white merchant class. There would be no corporate-dominated command economy, no bureaucratized welfare state, no crime-ridden urban ghettos, no prison-industrial complex, no police state, and no wave of political and economic refugees pouring across the border, no international imperial system or many of the other countless disasters facing America today.

Now let us imagine a scenario where the US federal regime miraculously and wonderfully disappears. That would be the end of the New World Order, dependent as it is on its principal benefactor in the person of the US federal state. No more foreign wars and imperialism, no more military-industrial complex, no more federal police state, no subsidies to corporate interests, no central banking scheme, no welfare state, no Department of Education, no media monopoly created by federal broadcast licensing schemes, no destruction of the economic and social infrastructure of local communities via federal "urban development" programs, no urban reservations of public housing, no federal highway system and its various accompanying subsidies, no federal drug war and prison system. Most of the major US corporations would collapse with production being taken over by workers, communities or local entrepreneurial groups. Stable local currencies backed by a precious metal standard would emerge. Control over the media would largely be localized. Schools, whether "public" or private, would be under local control. Military units would be dismantled, converted to local militias or contracted out as mercenaries. Federal Gestapo agents, such as those of the BATF or DEA, would have to get real jobs, assuming they were not killed in the upheaval.

What would the implications of all of this be for racial and cultural relations and immigration policy? The elimination of the welfare state and federal efforts to destroy urban economic life and social fabrics would, over time, bring about increased self-sufficiency and higher economic output for urban minority communities, with a subsequent reduction in crime and chaos. Federal laws prohibiting racial discrimination or implementing affirmative action programs would no longer exist, so whites could form racially homogenous communities and institutions if they wished. However, state activities that serve as a source of artificial privilege for whites would be eliminated. Many affluent whites obtain their positions by staffing state and corporate bureaucracies that would disappear with the elimination of the state apparatus. So the combination of higher productivity by blacks and fewer entitlements for whites would tend to equalize the overall distribution of economic resources among the racial groups. Decentralization of local and regional political institutions would allow for the achievement of cultural sovereignty by many diverse groups. Instead of the countless lawsuits and endless debates about "rights" that transpire today, groups with different interests would simply go their own way rather that battle one another over the control of central power. Depending on local preferences, some schools would have prayers, sex education or bi-lingual education, others would not. Rural southern towns and counties might continue to honor their Confederate heritage. Separate black municipalities in urban areas might instead celebrate historic black leaders or African culture. Blacks who wished to do so could have their own schools where "Afro-centric" education was emphasized while whites might have schools with a "Euro-centric" orientation. Mutual trade and voluntary economic interaction would tend to harmonize overall social relations between divergent cultural groups.

What about immigration? This would largely be a local matter. Requirements for "citizenship" or "naturalization" would be determined according to community standards, as is currently the case in Switzerland. Immigration policies could be as restrictive as or as open-ended as local communities desired. There would be no federal entitlements to lure immigrants from poor nations to North America. There would be no federally imposed barriers to discrimination by those who did not wish to associate with newcomers. There would be no NAFTA-like arrangements to transport American jobs to nations with more readily exploitable labor. Indeed, under an economic order established largely on the principle of worker control of production, there would be no financial incentives for the type of disruptive "corporate globalization" currently taking place. American workers would not ship their own jobs overseas. Similarly, workers who control their own industries would not throw themselves out of work in order to employ cheap immigrant labor. Political and economic incentives for mass immigration would not be necessary. There would be no need for police state organizations such as the INS or the Border Patrol. Invasive immigration could be controlled by local militias.

On this last point, let me say that I recognize that many anarchists of the leftist variety view any and all forms of discrimination of a cultural or ethnic variety or all opposition to unlimited immigration to be a form of racist oppression. The hypocrisy of this position can be demonstrated easily enough. Let us imagine that tomorrow the entire population of New York City suddenly undergoes a mass conversion to anarcho-communism. The Big Apple is subsequently converted into a mass leftist-anarchist commune. What entry or residency requirements would be established for such a political body? Would any and all comers be welcome regardless of beliefs, behavior or economic output? Hardly. More likely members of those cultural groups considered conservative or reactionary would be expelled from the city along with those professing anarcho-communists someone, or anyone, accused of being racist, sexist, homophobic, producerist, transphobic, speciesist, et.al., and *ad nauseum*. If, for example, a group of neo-Nazi skinheads were to attempt a march in Central Park, certainly these anarchist believers in unlimited freedom would not impose formal censorship on such a display as they would be too busy beating the participants to death with baseball bats. Unfortunately, "anarchism" has its fair share of totalitarians. In their zeal to embrace bourgeois liberal pseudo-egalitarian monoculturalism, many anarchists have jettisoned such venerable anarchist traditions as decentralization, individual liberty, voluntary association, mutual aid (which can only occur among people with common interests and goals) and community autonomy. Instead, many anarchists have come to simply reflexively regurgitate the values and rhetoric of the left-wing of capital. Until this begins to change, anarchists will continue to remain a marginalized and irrelevant community.

Goodbye, Ultra-Leftism; Hello, Pan-Secessionism

For any movement or system of thought to remain relevant or dynamic, it must possess the internal capability of periodically reassessing its present course and shifting its focus and direction. Thus far, political anarchism has experienced two distinct stages. The first of these was the era of "classical" anarchism. Roughly defined, this was the period between the Marx/Bakunin split in the 1870s and the defeat of the Spanish anarchists in the 1930s. The second stage began during the 1960s with the emergence of a brand of anarchism that internalized the ideological framework of the New Left, and it is this framework that still prevails at the present time.

The classical anarchist movement was primarily oriented towards proletarian revolution and the historic labor movement. This was appropriate as the "labor question" was the principal political struggle of the time. The New Left-influenced anarchist movement ("neo-anarchism") oriented itself towards the movements that emerged during its own era. These included "anti-racism" (for instance, the movement against American and South African racial apartheid systems), "anti-colonialism" (opposition to the Vietnam War and other manifestations of imperialist aggression), "the women's movement" (second wave feminism), "gay liberation" (homosexuals were previously regarded as criminals, deviants or mentally ill by the wider society), the ecology movement, a variety of tendencies collectively known as "counterculturalism" and other comparable but lesser known movements, all of which had the purpose of challenging traditional institutions, systems of authority, social practices, cultural norms and so forth. The overwhelming majority of contemporary anarchists continue to function within this particular paradigm.

However, the question needs to be asked as to whether this paradigm is really appropriate in the early 21st century. If it were found to be inappropriate, what might the alternative be? In more recent times, a number of tendencies have emerged within the anarchist milieu that challenged the dominant New Left-derived paradigm. These include primitivists, eco-anarchists, anarcho-capitalists, anarcho-monarchists, national-anarchists, tribal anarchists, anarcho-pluralists, a variety of ideologies that might be collectively labeled "free-market anti-capitalists," post-left anarchists, Christian anarchists, and a number of other perspectives. While there are significant differences between these tendencies, and each of these rejects the dominant New Left paradigm with varying degrees of consistency or fervor, collectively they compromise a dissident force within anarchism that seeks to move past the current second stage in the history of anarchism and into a new era.

The two most serious weaknesses of contemporary anarchism are illustrated by the opening paragraph of the Wikipedia entry on anarchism:

> *Anarchism is a political philosophy encompassing theories and attitudes which consider the state, as compulsory government, to be unnecessary, harmful, and/or undesirable, and favors the absence of the state (anarchy.)Specific anarchists may have additional criteria for what constitutes anarchism, and they often disagree with each other on what these criteria are. According to the Oxford Companion to Philosophy "there is no single defining position that all anarchists hold, and those considered anarchists at best share a certain family resemblance."*

Among many contemporary anarchists, there is an observable tendency to ignore the struggle against the state, or to treat the battle against the state as only one matter on a laundry list of preferred causes, usually those of a conventionally leftist or countercultural nature. This is the first weakness. The other is the matter of sectarianism, i.e., setting an amount of "additional criteria for what constitutes anarchism" that is so large that it becomes self-defeating when it comes to the matter of building an actual movement that can wield political influence.

There needs to be a revolution within the anarchist movement itself. This should be a revolution that re-orients the anarchist movement towards the primary anarchist objective of state abolitionism. Second, there needs to be a shift in contemporary anarchist thought and action that involves a retreat from the current tunnel-visioned focus on ultra-leftism and counterculturalism. A new focus that is broader and that speaks to a wider variety of issues and population groups is necessary. Third, there needs to be an evaluation of tactics, and the adoption of new tactics that are relevant to current political realities.

If one examines the historic anarchist communities from the past, one thing that is immediately noticeable about these anarchist polities from the past is how different many of them were from one another. Consequently, it is probable that in a civilization where anarchist communities became widespread there would be wide variation in the specific ideological, cultural or structural content of these communities. This automatically means that the sectarian differences between competing strands within anarchism are irrelevant. Different kinds of anarchists will form different kinds of communities in those geographical regions where their own tendencies are prevalent. For instance, anarcho-communists and anarcho-capitalists, leftist anti-racist anarchists and national-anarchists, anarcho-futurists and primitivists, gay anarchists and Christian anarchists, anarcha-feminists and anarcho-monarchists, may not even consider one another to be "true" anarchists, but these battles simply do not matter if different kinds of anarchists are simply "doing their own thing" within the context of their own communities, institutions and organizations.

How, in a nation-state like the United States, could an anarchist movement become large enough, or influential or powerful enough, to actually carry out a revolution rivaling that of, for instance, the Spanish anarchists of the 1930s? Clearly the anarchist movement in North America could never do such a thing, given its small size and narrow focus. But what about a much larger popular movement, in which anarchists assume leadership roles, and with a much broader focus than what is found in the anarchist milieu at present?

The military historian Martin Van Creveld has written about the present decline of the state as an institution, and there are a number of possible scenarios that may eventually bring about the downfall of the American regime itself. Americans are in the process of sorting themselves out into communities specifically oriented towards their own political, cultural or lifestyle interests. Opinion polls have demonstrated the amount of support for secessionist movements in the U.S., and the surprising nature of these numbers. A number of relatively recent works by serious scholars offer us an alternative economic paradigm beyond the standard "big business vs. big government" false dichotomy.

My friends, these works contain the ideas and information necessary to develop a popular revolutionary movement in North America. This essay is an attempt to synthesize these ideas and develop a comprehensive strategy for their application. No single reader is likely to agree with every argument or position taken in that essay, but its purpose is to "get the ball rolling" concerning the debate as to how anarchist revolution in North America will actually be carried out.

The single idea of state abolitionism will never be popular enough to become a mass movement. Most people simply are not that averse to political authority. However, the idea of secession has its roots in American history, culture and tradition. Therefore, anarchists should simply work to develop their own independent enclaves reflecting the value systems of their particular sect of anarchism, encourage other secession movements, and work to popularize the idea of secession. An effort should be made to appeal to those demographic groups most under attack by the state, those with single issues that put them in conflict with the state, and those who have the least to lose and most to gain by rejecting the state.

Further, anarchists should position themselves as the upholders of the economic interests of ordinary people. Opinion polls indicate that the issues of most concern to the public at large at present are unemployment, government spending and healthcare. What, if anything, do anarchists plan to do about these matters? How many individual anarchists have even given any thought to such topics? If you do not like the ideas that have been mentioned thus far, then come up with something of your own.

Particularly problematic is the question of people and groups with polarized opposite views on many issues participating in the same movement. For instance, the conflicts between the various anarchist sects (Anarchist People of Color and Crimethinc come immediately to mind), or the conflict between secessionists holding opposing cultural or ideological perspectives. No doubt, there are some people who will not enter into a movement that includes others with whom they strongly disagree on certain questions no matter what. These individuals will simply have to fall by the wayside. The proper response to such questions is the "good riddance" argument. In a decentralized political system, with voluntary association and community autonomy, leftist anti-racist anarchists and national-anarchists need not have any association with one another, nor anarcho-capitalists and anarcho-communists, nor gays and religious conservatives, nor racists and racial minorities, nor snobby rich people and slummy poor people, nor druggies and straight edges, nor feminists and male chauvinist pigs, nor Crimethinc and Anarchist People of Color. Everyone wins but the state, the ruling class, and the empire.

The New Anarchist
Movement is Growing

In recent years, I have noticed that the number of people accepting the label of "anarchist" for their political identity has grown considerably. Equally important is that I have also noticed that an increasing number of people who identify as anarchists are beginning to reject the leftist fanaticism that has dominated much of the anarchist milieu for decades.

Of course, sectarian left-anarchism or anarcho-communism is not the only form of anarchist sectarianism. Anarcho-capitalists, the left-libertarian mutualists, primitivists, "lifestyle" anarchists and others can and do embrace doctrinaire and exclusionary positions at times. However, even sectarians in these camps have the collective impact of diluting the sectarian leftist tendencies or undermining their general level of influence.

This is a necessary transitional development to a more effective form of anarchism. Because I am known for being highly critical of the anarchist milieu in many ways, I am occasionally asked what I think an ideal anarchist movement would look like. Of course, I have written a voluminous amount of material outlining my views on this question (and even then what I have written thus far is complete). But I have also found that the heterodox and eclectic approach that I take to anarchist theory and strategy is overly confusing or complicated for many casual readers. So here are the basics of my approach in a nutshell.

The new anarchist movement would embrace the many scattered tribes and sects of anarchism (all of the hyphenated tendencies that you can read about in a standard book or

Wikipedia article about anarchism). This would include left and right, as well as "neither fish nor fowl." tendencies among anarchists. All of the many anarchist tendencies would continue to emphasize projects related to their primary social issues, identity groups, or preferred economic systems, but with the overarching goal of created decentralized societies with diverse and self-managed communities.

The new anarchist movement would generally shun insisting that all anarchists and other radicals adopt the most fanatically leftist views possible on topical issues. Instead, the new anarchist movement would recognize that issues involving standard public controversies such as the environment, race, gender, religion, immigration, economics, guns, sex, abortion, animal rights, euthanasia, etc. etc. etc. are complicated issues on which reasonable, honest, and well-intentioned people can disagree. In the spirit of Voltaire, the new anarchist movement would encourage open and honest debate on such questions with a fair hearing for all contending points of view.

This does not mean that any sub grouping of anarchists needs to renounce their beliefs or activism regarding any particular issue. The new anarchist movement would certainly include black anarchists organizing against police brutality, anarcho-syndicalists engaged in labor organizing, eco-anarchists engaged in environmental activism, feminist and LGBT anarchists organizing on behalf of their own communities, native or indigenous anarchists organizing to obtain rights to their historic lands, non-schoolers agitating against compulsory education laws, youth rights activists organizing against the drinking age and police harassment, anarcho-pacifists protesting military bases, anarcho-libertarians protesting taxes, anti-fascists protesting fascist organizations, neo-reactionary anarcho-capitalists protesting social justice warriors, pro-Palestinians organizing boycotts of Israel, animal rights activists protesting fur or factory farming, pro-lifers protesting abortion clinics, pro-choicers protesting pro-lifers, LGBTs protesting Westboro

Baptist Church, MRAs protesting feminists, feminists protesting MRAs, race-realist protesting antifas, sex worker rights activists organizing against vice laws, counterculturalists organizing against drug laws, prisoner rights activists agitating against the prison-industrial complex, militia men protesting gun laws, sovereign citizens protesting driver's licenses, etc. etc. etc. etc.

Ultimately, however, there needs to be some kind of collective resistance to the institutions of mass murder, mass imprisonment, and mass impoverishment that currently rule over everyone, and realistic means of dealing with genuine and irreconcilable conflicts between polarized social and political groups.

As for dealing with conflict within the anarchist movement, and within the wider society as well, the new anarchist movement would appeal to and apply conventional anarchist principles such as free association, decentralization, federalism, secession, voluntaryism, and pluralism. Towards this end, the new anarchist movement would work to build united revolutionary fronts against the overarching institutions of imperialism, plutocracy, and statism that have come to dominate mainstream societies, and work to develop a society-wide consensus towards the dissolution of concentrated power into regional federations and independent municipalities. This would mean working to build relationships with decentralizing tendencies across the political and cultural spectrum.

This is not to say that all dissident opinion is compatible with anarchistic or even libertarian values. But the threat posed by authoritarian dissidents, whether communists, fascists, or theocrats should be evaluated on the basis of to what degree these actually have the capacity to achieve state power. At present, neo-Nazi, Marxist-Leninist, and Islamist groups exist only on the margins of the liberal democratic nations. With the possible exception of Golden Dawn, there are no totalitarian revolutionary parties that even hold seats in the parliaments of any Western nations. The primary enemies of anarchists in these nations are the neo-liberal and neo-conservative state-capitalists who actually control these regimes, and that is where the energies of anarchists should be focused. Meanwhile, we should utilize every forum possible to advance our own views.

Is Market Anarchism Eclipsing Marxist-Anarchism?

It seems to me that in the last couple of years "free market anarchism" in its various forms has grown to the point where it's now starting to eclipse or even surpass the "anarcho-Marxists" in terms of size and influence. I base this observation on the number of public events sponsored by both, and the online presence of both. Am I right or wrong in this perception?

I ask not because I think either the anarcho-Marxists or the mainstreams libertarians are genuinely radical or revolutionary movements for the most parts, but because I'm interested in what the prevailing ideological currents are at present. It seems to me the anarcho-Marxists are in the process of self-destructing. It's getting to where every time they hold a public meeting a fight breaks out between rival PC factions which, ironically, results in the cops often being called. I don't see a movement like that ever growing or sustaining itself because it's so ineffective at organizing, maintaining present participants, or recruiting new ones. In my view, the anarcho-Marxists cannot self-destruct soon enough. I say that for functional and strategic reasons rather than ideological ones. They're a collection of dysfunctional overgrown 12 year olds who are a barrier to the development of a more genuinely radical movement with an anarchist orientation. If "free market anarchism" were to eclipse them, it would simply be a matter of eliminating one obstacle that's presently in the way.

This is not to say that there are not also many problems within libertarianism/market anarchism. With the growth of libertarianism in recent years, it seems like it is being pulled towards efforts at co-optation from two main directions. One of these is obviously the corporate-oriented right wing, e.g. Americans for Prosperity, Freedom Works, etc. The other is the PC Left, e.g. C4SS, BHL, Reisenwitz, etc. All of that is to be expected. Much of libertarianism is just a microcosm of the wider society. The left wing of libertarianism is Democrats under another name, and the right wings of libertarianism are Republicans under another name. Indeed, at present there seems to be civil war going on among libertarians/market anarchists between the brutalists and the bleeding hearts is a way that's reflective of the mainstream "culture wars" that represent rivalries among elite and/or middle class factions, and that are irrelevant to actual revolutionary struggle.

Opposition to US imperialism has to be the flagship issue of any serious radical movement in North America, and not arguing about mainstream issues. Anyone who wants to soft pedal anti-imperialism or water it down, much less compromise with the empire, is out of the game before it begins. Whenever I encounter any purported "radical" movement, organization, or individual, the first thing I usually ask is how they feel about breaking up the USA into smaller political units. If they express opposition, then I know they're already out of the game. I'll then ask how they would feel about achieving such through capital "R" Revolutionary action. If they don't recoil in horror, then I'll assume maybe they have some potential.

Why I am an Anarcho-Pluralist, Part I

Over the last few days, there's been an interesting discussion of left-libertarian philosopher Charles Johnson (also known as "Rad Geek"). The subject matter of the discussion provides a very good illustration of why any sort of libertarian philosophy that demands a rigid universalism cannot work in practice. A poster called "Soviet Onion" remarks:

> It seems that both social anarchism and market libertarianism have respectively come to adopt forms of collectivism typical of either the statist left or right. That's a result of the perceived cultural affinity they have with those larger groups, and partly also a function of the fact that they appeal to people of different backgrounds, priorities and sentiments (and these two factors tend to reinforce each other in a cyclical way, with new recruits further entrenching the internal movement culture and how it will be perceived by the following generation of recruits).

> On the "left" you have generic localists who feel that altruism entails loyalty to the people in immediate proximity (they'll unusually use the term "organic community" to make it seem more natural and thus unquestionably legitimate). Most of them are former Marxists and social democrats, this is simply a way to recast communitarian obligations and tacitly authoritarian sentiments under the aegis of "community" rather than "state". This comes as an obvious result of classical anarchism being eclipsed as THE radical socialist alternative by Leninism for most of the twentieth century. Now that it's once again on the rise, it's attracting people who would have otherwise been state-socialists, and who carry that baggage with them when they cross over.

On the "right", it's a little more straightforward. Libertarians have adopted the conservative "State's Rights" kind of localism as a holdover from their alliance with conservatives against Communism, to the point that it doesn't even matter if the quality of freedom under that state is worse than the national average, just so long as it's not the Federal Government. And with this, any claim to moral universality, or the utilitarian case for decentralism go right out the window. Like true parochialism, it hates the foreign and big just because it is foreign and big.

That's also one of the reasons why I think there's a division between "social" and "market" anarchists; they each sense that they come from different political meta-groups and proceed from a different set of priorities; the established gap between right and left feels bigger than the gap between them and statists of their own variety. And the dogmatisms that say "we have to support the welfare state, workplace regulations and environmental laws until capitalism is abolished" or "we should vote Republican to keep taxes down and preserve school choice" are as much after-the-fact rationalizations of this feeling as they are honest attempts at practical assessment.

The problem with left-libertarianism (or with the 21st century rebirth and recasting of 19th century individualism, if you want to imperfectly characterize it that way), is that instead of trying to transcend harmful notions of localism, it simply switches federalism for communitarianism. It does this partially as an attempt to ingratiate itself to social anarchists, and partly because, like social anarchists, it recognizes that this idea is superficially more compatible with an anti-state position. But it also neglects the social anarchists' cultural sensibilities; hence the more lax attitude toward things like National Anarchism.

These are some very insightful comments. And what do they illustrate? That human beings, even professed "anarchists," are in fact tribal creatures, and by extension follow the norms of either their tribe of origin or their adopted tribe, and generally express more sympathy and feel a stronger sense of identification with others who share their tribal values (racism, anti-racism, feminism, family, homosexuality, homophobia, religion, atheism, middle class values, underclass values, commerce, socialism) than they do with those with whom they share mere abstractions ("anarchy," "liberty," "freedom").

Last year, a survey of world opinion indicated that it is the Chinese who hold their particular society in the highest regard, with 86 percent of Chinese expressing satisfaction with their country. Russians expressed a 54 percent satisfaction rate, and Americans only 23 percent. Observing these numbers, Pat Buchanan remarked:

"Yet, China has a regime that punishes dissent, severely restricts freedom, persecutes Christians and all faiths that call for worship of a God higher than the state, brutally represses Tibetans and Uyghur's, swamps their native lands with Han Chinese to bury their cultures and threatens Taiwan."

"Of the largest nations on earth, the two that today most satisfy the desires of their peoples are the most authoritarian."

What are we to make of this? That human beings value security, order, sustenance, prosperity, collective identity, tribal values and national power much more frequently and on a deeper level than they value liberty. Of course, some libertarians will likely drag out hoary Marxist concepts like "false consciousness" or psycho-babble like "Stockholm syndrome" to explain this, but it would be more helpful to simply face the truth: That liberty is something most people simply don't give a damn about.

Why I am an Anarcho-Pluralist, Part I

The evidence is overwhelming that most people by nature are inclined to be submissive to authority. The exceptions are when the hunger pains start catching up with them and their physical survival is threatened, or when they perceive their immediate reference groups (family, religion, culture, and tribe) as being under attack by authority. We see this in the political expressions of America's contemporary "culture wars." During the Clinton era, many social or cultural conservatives and religious traditionalists regarded the U.S. regime as a tyranny that merited armed revolt. During the Bush era such rhetoric disappeared from the Right, even though Bush expanded rather than rolled back the police state. Meanwhile, liberals who would denounce Bush as a fascist express polar opposite sentiments towards the Obama regime, even though policies established by Bush administration have largely continued. So how do we respond to this? Soviet Onion offers some suggestions:

> The proper position for us, and what could really set us apart from everyone and make us a more unique and consistent voice for individualism in the global Agora, is to recognize all cultures as nothing more than mimetic prisons and always champion the unique and nonconforming against the arbitrary limitations that surround them, recognizing their destruction as barriers in the sense of being normative. And to that end there's the instrumental insight that the free trade, competition, open movement and open communication are forces that pry open closed societies, not by force, but by giving those who chafe under them so many options to run to that they make control obsolete, and thus weaken control's tenability as a foundation on which societies can reasonably base themselves. Think of it as "cultural Friedmanism": the tenet that open economies dissolve social authority the same way they render political authority untenable.

THAT's what left-libertarianism needs to be about, not some half-baked federation of autarkic Southern towns filled with organic farms and worker co-operatives. It can still favor these things, but with a deeper grounding. It doesn't ignore patriarchy, racism, heterosexism, but opposes them with a different and more consistent understanding of what liberation means.

But how far should our always championing of the "unique and nonconforming" go? If a group of renegades were to show up at the workers' cooperatives one day, and take over the place should anarchists simply say, "Hell, yeah, way to go, non-conformists." As for the question of the "Big Three" among left-wing sins ("racism, sexism and homophobia"), are we to demand that every last person on earth adopt the orthodox liberal position on these issues as defined by the intellectual classes in post-1968 American and Western Europe? Why stop at "patriarchy, racism and heterosexism"? Soviet Onion points out that many "left-wing" anarchists do not stop at that point:

I used to be an anarcho-communist. Actually, I started out as someone who was vaguely sympathetic to mainstream libertarianism but could never fully embrace it due to the perceived economic implications. I eventually drifted to social anarchism thanks to someone whose name I won't mention, because it's too embarrassing.

After hanging around them for a while I realized that, for all their pretenses, most of them were really just state-socialists who wanted to abolish the State by making it smaller and calling it something else. After about a year of hanging around Libcom and the livejournal anarchist community, I encountered people who, under the aegis of "community self-management", supported

• smoking and alcohol bans

• bans on currently illicit drugs

• bans on caffeinated substances (all drugs are really just

preventing you from dealing with problems, you see)

- censorship of pornography (on feminist grounds)

- sexual practices like BDSM (same grounds, no matter the gender of the participants or who was in what role)

- bans on prostitution (same grounds)

- bans on religion or public religious expression (this included atheist religions like Buddhism, which were the same thing because they were "irrational")

- bans on advertisement (which in this context meant any free speech with a commercial twist)

- bans on eating meat

- gun control (except for members of the official community-approved militia, which is in no way the same thing as a local police department)

- mandatory work assignments (i.e. slavery)

- the blatant statement, in these exact words, that "Anarchism is not individualist" on no less than twelve separate occasions over the course of seven months. Not everybody in those communities actively agreed with them, but nobody got up and seriously disputed it.

- that if you don't like any of these rules, you're not free to just quit the community, draw a line around your house and choose not to obey while forfeiting any benefits. No, as long as you're in what they say are the the boundaries (borders?) of "the community", you're bound to follow the rules, otherwise you have to move someplace else ("love it or leave it", as the conservative mantra goes). You'd think for a moment that this conflicts with An-com property conceptions because they're effectively exercising power over land that they do not occupy, implying that they own it and making "the community" into One Big Landlord a la Hoppean feudalism

So I decided that we really didn't want the same things, and that what they wanted was really some kind of Maoist concentration commune where we all sit in a circle and publicly harass the people who aren't conforming hard enough. No thanks, comrade.

These left-wing anarchists sound an awful lot like right-wing Christian fundamentalists or Islamic theocrats. Nick Manley adds:

I have encountered an "anarchist" proponent of the draft on a directly democratic communal level.

Of course, we also have to consider all of the many other issues that anarchists and libertarians disagree about: abortion, immigration, property theory, economic arrangements, and children's' rights, animal rights, environmentalism, just war theory, and much, much else. We also have to consider that anarchists and libertarians collectively are a very small percentage of humanity. Nick Manley says:

I spend more time around libertarians then left-anarchists — although, I briefly entered "their" world and sort of know some of them around here. I was a left-anarchist at one time, but I no longer feel comfortable with the hardcore communalism associated with the ideology. I don't really want to go to endless neighborhood meetings where majorities impose their will on minorities. I also would agree with Adam Reed that it's naive to imagine such communes being free places in today's world — perhaps, this is less true of New Zealand.

The list of things supported by anarcho-communists posted by Soviet Onion confirms my fears about village fascism posturing as "anti-statism". I frankly do just want to be left alone in my metaphorical "castle" — I say metaphorical, because I am not an atomist and don't live as such. I will engage in social activities, but I will not allow someone to garner my support through the use of force or do so to others. Like Charles, I have a strong emotional and intellectually principled revulsion to aiding the cause of statism in any way whatsoever. I'd be much happier being at some risk of death from handguns then in enforcing laws that harm entirely well intentioned peaceful people. This is not a mere political issue for me. I know more than a few people with guns who deserve no prison time whatsoever — one of them has guns affected by the assault weapons ban.

I honestly see a lot of principled parallels between conservative lifestyle tribalism and left-liberal lifestyle tribalism. Oh yes: there are contextual inductive distinctions to be made. A gun is not the same as homosexuality. The collectivist dynamic is still the same. Gun owners become no longer human in sense of rational beings. All of contemporary politics seems to be one thinly veiled civil war between fearful tribalists.

It would appear that tribalism is all that we have. I have been through a long journey on this question. I was a child of the Christian Right, drifted to the radical Left as a young man, then towards mainstream libertarianism, then the militia movement and the populist right, along the way developing the view that the only workable kind of libertarianism would be some kind of pluralistic but anti-universalist, decentralized particularism. Rival tribes who are simply incompatible with one another should simply have their own separatist enclaves. Unlike the other kinds of libertarianism, there is actually some precedent for what I'm describing to be found in past cultures. As Thomas Naylor remarks:

Conservatives don't want anyone messing with the distribution of income and wealth. They like things the way they are. Liberals want the government to decide what is fair. Liberals believe in multiculturalism, affirmative action, and minority rights. Conservatives favor states' rights over minority rights.

What liberals and conservatives have in common is that they are both into having—owning, possessing, controlling, and manipulating money, power, people, material wealth, and things. Having is one of the ways Americans deal with the human condition—separation, meaninglessness, powerlessness, and death. To illustrate how irrelevant the terms "liberal" and "conservative" have become, consider the case of Sweden and Switzerland, two of the most prosperous countries in the world.

Sweden is the stereotypical democratic socialist state with a strong central government, relatively high taxes, a broad social welfare net financed by the State, and a strong social conscience. Switzerland is the most free market country in the world, with the weakest central government, and the most decentralized social welfare system. Both are affluent, clean, green, healthy, well-educated, democratic, nonviolent, politically neutral, and among the most sustainable nations in all of history. By U.S. standards, they are both tiny. Switzerland and Sweden work, not because of political ideology, but rather because the politics of human scale always trumps the politics of the left and the politics of the right. Under the politics of human scale, a politics that trumps our now-outdated and useless "liberal-versus-conservative" dualistic mindset, there would be but one fundamental question: "Is it too big?"

It would seem that contemporary America is precisely the place to build a movement for this kind of decentralized particularism, a huge continent wide nation with many different cultures, religions, subcultures, ethnic groups and growing more diverse all the time, and where political and economic polarization is the highest it has been in over a century, and where dissatisfaction with the status quo is almost universal.

My challenge to anarchists, libertarians, communitarians, conservatives, radicals and progressives alike would be to ask yourself what kind of community you would actually want to live in, and where and how you would go about obtaining it. For instance, the geography of the culture war typically breaks down on the basis of counties, towns, precincts, municipalities and congressional districts rather than states or large regions. So why not envision forming a community for yourself and others in some particular locality that is consistent with your own cultural, economic or ideological orientation? The Free State Project, Christian Exodus, Second Vermont Republic, Green Panthers and Twin Oaks Commune are already doing this.

Political victory in the United States is achieved through the assembling of coalitions of narrow interest groups who often have little in common with one another (gun toting rednecks and country club Republicans, homosexuals and traditional working class union Democrats). Imagine if a third force emerged in U.S. politics whose only unifying principle was a common desire to remove one's self and one's community from the system. The only thing anyone has to give up is the desire to tell other communities what to do.

Why I Am an Anarcho-Pluralist, Part II

Imagine, for one horribly unpleasant moment, that the anarchist movement (movements?) in North America, in their present form, were to carry out an actual revolution. What kind of social or political system would be the result? The Wikipedia entry on anarchism in the United States lists a number of individuals who represent North American anarchism in different ways. These include Michael Albert (Chomskyite proponent of participatory economics-"parecon"), Ashanti Alston (black power anarchist), Hakim Bey (lifestyle anarchist), Bob Black (nihilist and reputed psychopath), Kevin Carson (Proudhonian mutualist), Noam Chomsky (Marxo-syndicalist-anarcho-social democrat), Peter Coyote (love generation), Howard Ehrlich (social anarchist), David Friedman (anarcho-capitalist), David Graeber (anarcho-anthropologist), Hans-Hermann Hoppe (anarcho-monarchist), Derrick Jensen (primitivist), Jeff Luers (eco-anarchist prisoner), Judith Malina (anarcho-pacifist actress), the late James J. Martin (individualist anarchist and Holocaust revisionist), Wendy McElroy (Rothbardian anarcho-feminist individualist), Jason McQuinn (post-left anarchist), Cindy Milstein (Bookchinite), Chuck Munson (anarchist without adjectives), Joe Peacott (individualist-anarchist), Sharon Presley (left-libertarian feminist), Keith Preston (agent of the forces of darkness), Lew Rockwell (Rothbardian paleolibertarian), Jeremy Sapienza (market anarchist), Crispin Sartwell (individualist-anarchist), Rebecca Solnit (environmentalist), Starhawk (neo-pagan eco-feminist), Warcry (eco-anarchist), Dana Ward (anarcho-archivist), David Watson (primitivist), Mike Webb (murder victim), Fred Woodworth (atheist anarchist), John Zerzan (primitivist) and Howard Zinn (New Left anarcho-Marxist).

Why I Am an Anarcho-Pluralist, Part II

This list does not even begin to mention all of the ideological tendencies to be found among anarchists, e.g., indigenous anarchism, anarcho-communism, national-anarchism, insurrectionary anarchism, Christian anarchism and many others. Even so, anarchists collectively probably do not comprise even one percent of the population at large. Imagine if the anarchist milieu were to grow to include tens of millions of people. Most likely all of these specific tendencies would grow exponentially, and some new ones no one has heard of yet would probably appear. How would anarchists go about organizing society if indeed anarchism was to become a mass movement and the state in its present form was to disappear. More specifically, how would we reconcile the differences between all of these different tendencies, and how would anarchists co-exist with persons of other belief systems? Unless we want to start sending people to re-education camps, or placing them in gulags, or engaging in summary or mass executions we had better start thinking some of this out.

There are really only three ways. One would be anarcho-totalitarianism, where whatever anarchist faction or group of factions that happens to have the most power simply represses their rivals, anarchists and non-anarchists alike. Another would be anarcho-mass democracy, where we have an anarchist parliament consisting of the Syndicalist Party, Primitivist Party, Libertarian Party, Ecology Party, Feminist Party, et.al., perhaps presided over by, say, Prime Minister Chuck Munson. While this might be an interesting situation, it ultimately wouldn't be much different than the kinds of states we have today.

The only other alternative is the dispersion of power to local units. These could be localities where everything is completely privatized (Hoppe) or everything is completely collectivized (anarcho-communism), or some point in between. The specific anarchist tendencies these communities represented would be determined according to prevailing ideological currents at the local level. One contemporary anarchist observes:

The Failure of Anarchism

The superficial story is that the primmies control the NW, the SW desert and the Appalachians, while the Reds control the entire NE block and have a mild advantage everywhere else.

So "after the revolution" the "primmies" would be dominant in their regions and the "Reds" in theirs, and presumably the Free Staters in theirs, and the queer anarchists in theirs, and so forth. It's also interesting to observe how radically different the value systems and definitions of "freedom" employed by different kinds of anarchists are. One anarchist has noted that some anarchists wish to bar alcohol, drugs, tobacco, meat, porn, S&M and prostitution from their communities. This should go along way with those libertarian-libertine anarchists for whom anarchy is synonymous with all sorts of legalized vice. Then there's the conflict between the ethno-preservationist national-anarchists and the anti-racist left-anarchists, and between the proprietarian anarchists and the communal anarchists. I've even come across an anarchist proponent of the draft. Of course, the different kinds of anarchists will insist that others are not *true* anarchists, but that's beside the point. Each of the different anarchist factions considers *themselves* to be the true anarchists, and that's not going to change.

The adherents of many of these philosophies act as though the fate of the world depends on their every move, when in reality each of these tendencies will often have no more than a few thousand, maybe a few hundred, maybe even just a few dozen sympathizers (or even fewer than that). Rarely is any attention given to the question of how anarchists will ever achieve any of their stated goals, to the degree that anarchists have any common goals, or any goals at all.

If anarchists want to have any impact on the wider society whatsoever, I believe there is only one way. First, anarchists whatever their other differences need to band together in a large enough number to become single-issue political pressure group. This would be a pressure group just like those in the mainstream: pro-choice, pro-life, pro-gun, anti-gun, pro-gay marriage, anti-gay marriage, marijuana decriminalization, etc. The purpose of this pressure group would be to reduce political authority down to lowest unit possible, which, I believe is the local community, i.e., cities, towns, villages, districts, neighborhoods, etc. I recognize some anarchists wish to reduce politics down to the individual level. I'm a little more skeptical of that. For instance, I'm not so sure competing criminal codes could exist in the same territorial jurisdiction, but I'm willing to agree to disagree on that. I say let's work to reduce things down to the city-state, county or village level, and then debate how much further to go from there. Such a pressure group could include not only anarchists of every kind, but also left-green decentralists, conservative local sovereignty groups, regionalist or secessionist tendencies or even good old fashioned Jeffersonian states' rightsers. This idea does not mean that every locality would need to be an independent nation unto itself. They could be sovereign entities within broader territorial confederations, so long as they retained their right of withdrawal or to veto policies favored by the larger bodies. This way, even communities with radically different cultural values or economic arrangements could collaborate on projects of mutual interest such as maintenance of transportation systems, firefighting, or common defense.

Meanwhile, outside the context of this single-issue movement for radical decentralization, the different anarchist factions could continue their other interests in different contexts. Libertarians could continue to push for private money or competing currencies. Syndicalists could continue to push for anarcho-syndicalist unions. Primitivists could set up tech-free communes or villages. Anti-racists could protest Klan marches, and national-anarchists could set up ethnic separatist intentional communities. Pro-lifers could agitate against abortion and feminists could agitate against pro-lifers. Gun nuts could simultaneously belong to the NRA and pacifists could belong to the Catholic Workers. Anarcho-communists could organize Israeli-style kibbutzim and anarcho-capitalists could set up their preferred private defense agencies.

Additionally, different factions with different beliefs could target certain geographical areas for colonization as the Free Staters are doing in New Hampshire, the Christian Exodus is doing in South Carolina, the Native Americans are doing in the Lakota Republic, or the Ron Paulistas are doing in the Liberty Districts. Indeed, Bill Bishop's interesting book "The Big Sort" describes how Americans are in the process of self-separation along the lines of culture, religion, ideology, political affiliation, sexuality, age, income, occupation and every conceivable other issue. Colonization can then become a movement for full-blown local secession. The values and ideals of those whom you disagree with are not as personally threatening if you do not have to live under the same political roof, and the worse someone's ideas are, the better that they be separate from everyone else.

This does not mean that sovereign communities cannot have institutionalized protects for individual liberties, minority rights, or popular rule. Some state constitutions or municipal charters already have protections of this type in some instances, and sometimes on a more expansive level than what is found in the U.S. Constitution. Individual sovereign communities could make such protections as extensive as they wanted. Nor does this mean that libertarian anti-statism is the "only" value. There are some values in life that transcend politics, and one can also be committed to other issues while also being committed to political decentralization and local sovereignty. For instance, I am also interested in prisoners' rights, legal, judicial, penal and police reform, ending the war on drugs, repealing consensual crime laws, abolishing compulsory school attendance laws, opposing zoning ordinances, eminent domain, the overregulation of land and housing markets, sex worker rights, the right to bear arms, self-defense rights, the rights of students, the homeless, the handicapped, medical patients and psychiatric inmates, freedom of speech and the press, labor organizing, worker cooperatives, mutual aid associations, home schools and alternative education, credit unions and mutual banks, LETS, land reform, indigenous peoples' rights, alternative media, non-state social services, and many other topics. My primary area of interest is foreign policy. In fact, foreign policy was the reason I became an anarchist and have remained one, in spite of being continually underwhelmed by the organized anarchist movement. I think the American empire and its effects on peoples throughout the world is an abomination, and I want to see it ended. Yet, I think at the same time an agglomeration of anarchist communities in North America would need some kind of "national defense" system, given that Europe and Asia may not "go anarchist" at the same moment, which is why I am interested in the paleoconservatives with their traditional American isolationist views.

At the same time, there are some topics that many anarchists are committed to that don't particularly interest me. Environmentalism is one of these. Like all reasonable people, I think we need clean air and water, and it's not cool to build a toxic waste dump in a residential area. Yet, the eco-doomsday ideologies associated with ideas like global warming and peak oil are not things I'm sold on as of yet. I also really just don't see what the big deal about endangered species is. The overwhelming majority of species that have existed thus far have already gone extinct, so what's a few more? Still, if this is an issue others care passionately about then by all means engage in direct action on behalf of sea turtles or spotted owls or against urban sprawl. Don't let me get in your way. Gay marriage is another topic I really just don't give a fuck about, not because I'm anti-gay but because I view marriage as an archaic religious and statist institution that anarchists or libertarians or radicals of any stripe should not be promoting. But that's just me. As an atheist, I also don't care much for the militant politicized atheism found in some circles. I agree that compulsory religious instruction and practice should not exist in state-run schools, but I think extending this idea to things like prayers at city council meetings or football games, or extracurricular religious clubs in state institutions, is taking things a bit far. It is this sort of thing that alienates the usually religious poor and working class from radicalism.

Lastly, we need to consider how to appeal to all those ordinary folks out there whose assistance we might need in order to achieve these kinds of goals. An anarchist-led, libertarian-populist, radical decentralist, pan-secessionist movement that appealed to the tradition and ideals of the American Revolution is the only possible avenue. What I have outlined here is essentially the same set of views promoted by Voltairine de Cleyre in her essays "Anarchism without Adjectives" and "Anarchism and American Traditions." If you don't like my views, then come up with a plan of your own and let the rest of us hear about it.

Why the Radical Left Should Consider Secession

Kirkpatrick Sale of the Middlebury Institute recently observed that there is presently "more attention being paid to secession than any time since 1865 and predicts that "one of the American states will vote for its independence in the next 10 years." Neo-secessionist sentiments are frequently stereotyped as a characteristic exhibited primarily by "right-wing extremists." Yet there are serious reasons why genuine progressives should consider secession. Among the most compelling reasons why the Left should consider dissolving the U.S. into multiple nations, regions, or city-states are:

- Break-up of the U.S.A. means an end to the American empire that has killed millions of people throughout the world over the last sixty-five years, including perhaps two million Iraqis, three million Southeast Asians, hundreds of thousands of Central Americans, half a million Timorese, thousands of Afghanis, and many, many more.

- Without the support of the U.S., international capitalist organizations such as the IMF, World Bank, WTO, etc. would be much less powerful and influential.

- The demise of the federal regime would mean an end to U.S. aid to Israel, and a fighting chance for the Palestinians.

- The collapse of the U.S. federal system would mean an end to federal corporate-welfare, bank-welfare, and, above all, the death of the military-industrial complex.

- No more federal regime means no more DHS, FBI, CIA, DEA, BATF, Bureau of Prisons, Bureau of Indian Affairs, federal drug war, federal mandatory minimums, or the national police state built up around the war on terrorism. What could be more successful at overturning the "terror war" legislation of the last eight years than complete disintegration of the federal government itself?

- An end to federal corporate welfare means a severe weakening of Big Pharma, agribusiness, or local developers utilizing federal money in efforts at gentrification.

- The disintegration of the U.S. means not only the end of federal drug prohibition but an end to U.S. support for the international drug war and the America-centric structure of international drug prohibition, thereby allowing other nations to develop more progressive policies on this matter.

Some may object that progressives have at times appealed to federal power against local reactionaries (for instance, in cases of civil rights, abortion rights, and church/state separation issues) and that dissolution of the federal regime may also weaken gains in this area. However, it should be considered that the majority of the U.S. population resides in the 75 to 100 largest urban, metropolitan areas. If these areas–New York, Washington D.C., Los Angeles, San Francisco, Portland, Chicago, Miami–were all independent city-states or micro nations along the lines of Monaco, Luxemburg, or Singapore, genuine progressives would be in a much superior political position than at present. The major U.S. urban areas tend to be the most diverse culturally, racially, ethnically, and religiously. It is also in these areas where the majority of racial minorities, LGBT people, persons with countercultural values, and those with left-leaning political views tend to be concentrated. The majority of the underclass persons fed into the prison-industrial complex also originate from the large cities. It is in the major cities where most abortion services are located and where most abortions take place.

If these larger urban areas were separated from the states in which they are presently located and from the federal system, urban progressives would no longer need to share space politically with rural, small-town, or suburban reactionaries, conservatives, or religious fundamentalists. Therefore, it would be immensely easier for independent city-states of this kind to enact, for instance, single-payer health care, same-sex marriage, stem cell research or a living wage. It would also be easier to protect abortion rights from the influence of current state legislatures or the federal government. Likewise, it would be much more possible to decriminalize drugs, prostitution, gambling and other "consensual crimes" along the lines of New Zealand, Portugal, or the Netherlands at present. Such changes would severely weaken and undermine the police state and prison-industrial complex.

The likely weakening of corporate power following the demise of federal and state corporate welfare would also provide a more level playing field for activists to take on landlords, developers, bankers, and other plutocratic interests on a municipal and regional level, and perhaps initiate economic alternatives like cooperatives, collectives, communes, LETS, mutuals, land trusts, and so forth. Meanwhile, social conservatives and other non-progressives who dissented from this prevailing liberal-libertarian-left paradigm could likewise achieve sovereignty for themselves in their exclusionary suburban enclaves, homogenous rural counties and towns, or sparsely populated red zones. Surely, this would be a better state of political affairs than the present system. If indeed secessionist sentiments are likely to grow in the years and decades ahead, why should progressives want to be left out of the action?

Pan-Anarchism: Its Basics and Its Relationship to Others

In the late nineteenth and early twentieth century, anarchism was the premiere revolutionary movement throughout both the Western world and in the pre-industrial world. For instance, even many contemporary anarchists do not realize that anarchism was about as large a movement in Latin America and China as it was in Europe. During the twentieth century, anarchism was eclipsed by other movements and ideologies for a variety of reasons. The economic and technological expansion of the twentieth century, along with population growth, helped to facilitate a general tendency towards centralization and bureaucratization (see James Burnham's "The Managerial Revolution"). The seeming "success" of the Bolshevik Revolution, the prestige of the Soviet Union, the appeal of Marxism to intellectuals, and influence of the Communist Parties helped to insure Communism's hegemony on the Left. Additionally, there was the defeat of the Anarchists in the Spanish Civil War, and escalating repression at the hands of communist, fascist, and capitalist regimes. Lastly, there was the growing tendency of many people to look towards the state as the means of alleviating the problems associated with capitalism, a tendency that proved to be an unprecedented disaster.

Anarchism slowly began resurgence in the late twentieth century due to the failures of Marxist states, and the growing influence of cultural radicalism, and anarchism has continued to grow in the twenty-first century while simultaneously exhibiting an increasing ideological diversity within its own ranks. Meanwhile, many of the same conditions that gave rise to the classical anarchist movement have started to reappear. As was the case during the nineteenth century and the period of the industrial

75

revolution, the present era of globalization has brought with it an unprecedented integration of markets, and an unprecedented expansion of technological capabilities, and yet the result of this has similarly been an unprecedented concentration of wealth and political power on an international scale. Consequently, class divisions have widened dramatically within both individual nations and between the Global North and the Global South. At the same time, American imperialism has achieved the level of global hegemony once held by British imperialism and the European colonial empires, and beyond.

Contemporary anarchism has continued to grow due to the rise of the anti-globalization movement, the "Occupy" movement, the anarchist youth culture and, in North America, the emergence of the various libertarian currents. Indeed, in the form of the Kurdish independence movement, led by the PKK, YPG, and YPG, anarchists now have a contemporary prototype for an anarchist revolution that parallels the anarchist insurgency led by the CNT-FAI of the Spanish Civil War.

American Revolutionary Vanguard and Attack the System were founded at the turn of the century for the purpose of reclaiming the position held by anarchism a century earlier as the world's principal revolutionary force, for unifying and synthesizing the various anarchist currents, for organizing resistance to U.S. imperialism within the mother country of the empire, for challenging the global plutocratic super class, for moving past the doctrinaire leftism of many contemporary anarchists, and for engaging in outreach and discussion with opposition movements from all across the political spectrum.

Pan-anarchism is oriented towards the purpose of opposing and overthrowing statism, capitalism, and imperialism, and replacing these with, for example, autonomous municipalities (Bookchin), decentralized cooperative economics (Proudhon), libertarian law codes based on the non-aggression principle (Spooner, Tucker, Rothbard), non-imperialist militia defense systems (PKK/

YPG/YPG and CNT/FAI), and self-determination for cultural, ethnic, and religious communities (Bakunin, Landauer, Rocker).

Pan-anarchism recognizes the legitimacy of the many different types of anarchism and prefers to emphasize the commonalities of these rather than their differences. Likewise, pan-anarchism regards the many differences of opinion among different types on anarchists on a wide range of topics to be a matter of in-house debate.

As for the relationship of pan-anarchism to other movements and ideologies, it might be argued that pan-anarchism is compatible with other movements and ideologies to the degree that these embrace some degree of libertarianism, decentralism, anti-authoritarianism, anti-statism, anti-capitalism, or anti-imperialism. For example, those wishing to form libertarian-capitalist "seasteads" are to a great degree compatible with pan-anarchism. Those wishing to form autonomous "neo-reactionary" city-states are to a great extent compatible with pan-anarchism. Those wishing to form religious communes functioning independently of liberal consumer society are compatible with pan-anarchism. Ordinary liberals or conservatives wishing to form regional independence or secessionist movements are likewise worthy of engagement and dialogue.

Pan-anarchism does not endorse one particular cultural model. While many anarchists have adopted a "hard left" cultural outlook, pan-anarchism does not regard this as necessary or mandatory, nor does pan-anarchism seek uniformity of agreement on ordinary contentious public issues, but instead encourages freedom of speech, inquiry, opinion, and association.

Lastly, pan-anarchism holds to a populist conception of political struggles in the form of the people versus the elite, the individual against the state, and the producers against the exploiters. The purpose of pan-anarchism is the formation of anarchist and populist federations on the local, regional, national, and international level for the purpose of carrying out revolutionary struggle.

The Rise and Fall of the Shining Path

Lessons for North American Insurgents

Throughout the 1980s, few guerrilla groups around the world were more feared or notorious than Peru's "Sendero Luminoso", or Shining Path. The group had its roots in a split from the Communist Party of Peru in the late 1960s led by a philosophy professor named Abimael Guzman, who provided an eccentric variation of Maoism as an ideological framework for the movement. Throughout the 1970s, Shining Path built a following for itself among student radicals in Peruvian universities. Around 1980, the group began an armed insurgency against the Peruvian government, having assembled its own militias in the process of its growth as a movement. Over the course of the next decade, Shining Path came to control much of the rural territory of Peru and began advancing towards the capital city of Lima. Despite its initial successes, the movement began to fall apart in the early 1990s.

A principal problem was the cult-like organizational structure of the Shining Path. A cult of personality had developed around Guzman and his capture in 1992 had the effect of decapitating the insurgency. Another issue was the alienation of the peasant population from the insurgency due to its disrespect for the traditional culture of rural Peru and the extreme brutality of Shining Path attacks on its perceived enemies, the ranks of whom included rival leftists and community organizers as well as the Peruvian ruling class and government itself. The alienation grew to such a degree that the peasants would often back the government's efforts to repress the insurgency until the government's atrocities began to overshadow even those of the Shining Path. What can North American radicals learn from the example of the Shining Path? There are two essential lessons. First, an organizational structure that is capable of surviving the death, capture or incapacitation of its leadership is indispensible. An interesting example of this is the Nuestra Familia crime syndicate which thrives in spite of the incarceration of all of its leaders in maximum security American prisons, in complete isolation from one another. While leadership itself cannot simply be done away with, the body of the insurgency must be able to operate even in the absence of the head. The organizational structure commonly referred to as "leaderless resistance" would appear to be the appropriate model, with individual militants operating within the context of clandestine networks set up for the purpose of sharing intelligence and coordinating mutual activities.

Another important issue is the necessity of maintaining an attitude of respect for the institutions and cultures of local peoples. Ordinary Americans may well look the other way when System Pigs and their stooges become targets so long as they do not feel threatened in the process. However, "citizens" will not accept violent crimes committed against ordinary persons or threats to their livelihoods or things that they hold sacred (for example, affronts to their various religions). As the insurgent militia, paramilitary and guerrilla organizations evolve in the United States and Canada, and as the armed struggle commences, it will be essential that the insurgents conduct themselves properly within the territories that fall under rebel control. The best plan is to simply leave ordinary people alone and let them go about their business, in the process seizing the holdings of enemy governmental and corporate institutions and placing them under popular control and setting up common law courts or arbitration panels for the sake of settling disputes arising from common crimes or economic rivalries. Unnecessary massacres of the type that occurred at Oklahoma City or the World Trade Center should be avoided at all costs in order to prevent popular alienation. The average Joe needs to believe that he is either better off, or at least no worse off, under the rule of the insurgents than under the rule of the present regime.

The elimination of the present regime should occur with as little disruption in the daily lives of ordinary people as possible. Electrical and other utility services should continue except in cases of military emergency. Television and radio programming should continue to operate on schedule except where necessary to silence enemy propaganda or communications systems. The ideal situation would be one where everyday people continue to go about their business, traveling about from work to school to the grocery store to the beauty salon to the drinking hole and so on, all the while the insurgents are pulling the rug out from under the System Pigs, shutting down police departments in favor of revolutionary militias, eliminating the state's court system in favor of our own common law courts, releasing prisoners and eradicating the prison-industrial complex, turning corporate operations over to consumer coops, dismantling enemy governments and setting up our own revolutionary councils, allowing different cultural, religious and ethnic factions to go their own way and form their own private associations, seizing military bases, armories and nuclear silos and shutting down the imperial war machine and stripping federal, state and municipal treasuries in order to provide reparations or severance compensation to prisoners, social security recipients, dislocated military, police or low-level corporate or bureaucratic workers, and some kind of settlement to America's historical racial/ethnic conflicts.

It can be expected that the end-product of such a revolution would be quite "liberal" in the traditional Jeffersonian, as opposed to modern totalitarian, sense. The general level of individual freedom would be considerably higher than at present. However, there might also be a proliferation of a number of relatively or intensely closed communities, particularly among those operating within the framework of some sort of racial, religious or cultural exclusionism or some sort of overtly authoritarian political ideology. Sparta will have to co-exist with Athens and the Puritans will have to co-exist with the Libertines, pluralistically when possible, spatially segregated when not. Furthermore, the majority of the population of North America will not be part of the revolution. The Radical Alliance, even transcending the traditional boundaries of Left and Right, will still be a minority, although a militant minority that is subsequently able to obtain power way beyond its numbers (like present-day Zionists). Therefore, co-existence between citizens and radicals will also be necessary. A polycentric network of governmental, economic, educational and legal institutions will be needed in order to accommodate such divergent interests and separate conflicting elements from one another for the sake of preserving the social peace and avoiding counterrevolution. Following the Revolution, there will likely be a new insurgency launched by remnants of the former regime that could result in a civil war that would last for decades. The achievement of ultimate victory by the Revolution will require political leadership of the highest caliber on the part of the revolutionaries. The System Pigs are primarily fools and incompetents, and their counterrevolutionary efforts would likely be inept and involve considerable terrorism against civilian targets. The citizens must come to realize that Anarchist rule will be "just" and "tolerant" as conventionally defined, indeed even more so. Ultimately, we must also win the war for "hearts and minds", not because we are do-gooders or humanists, but because we are faithful Machiavellians.

Rightism without Jingoism, Leftism without Political Correctness

Martin Van Creveld's masterful work "The Rise and Decline of the State" argues that the nation-state system as it has been known since the time of the 1648 Treaty of Westphalia is on its way out. As the twenty-first century progresses, conventional states of the kind that began to emerge several centuries ago and fully established themselves in the 19th and 20th centuries will be challenged by regional autonomist movements, transnational federations, separatist breakaway movements and fourth generation private armies and sources of authority outside the state.

If this is true, then the next wave of political radicalism will be the precise opposite of the radicalisms that arose in the 18th, 19th and 20th centuries-liberalism, socialism and nationalism-all of which aimed towards more concentrated political authority. More than a century and a half since Proudhon first proclaimed himself an anarchist it is time for anarchism to achieve its moment in the sun. What would a 21st century revolutionary anarchism look like?

1. It would draw on the history of classical anarchism and other pre-existing forms of anarchism, but modify these to make them more compatible with the times.

2. It would attack the Left, i.e., Liberalism and Marxism, as its primary enemies, particularly in North America, given that North America has no historical attachment to the Ancient Regime and the traditional Right. Instead, the enemy to be assaulted is modern bourgeoisie liberalism (internationalist, social democratic, corporatist, multiculturalist, therapeutic, managerialist)

3. It would specifically embrace movements, causes and groups ignored by the Left establishment, focusing primarily on the lumpenproletariat, petite bourgeoisie, rural agricultural population and the déclassé elements from all class backgrounds.

4. It would crossover to the radical Middle with a populist-decentralist economic outlook standing in opposition to both Big Government and Big Business.

5. It would crossover to the vast culture of right-wing populism recognizing the many economic, foreign policy, civil liberties, decentralist and cultural rights issues raised by these milieus.

6. Its primary strategy would be the creation of alliance of local and regional secession movements spanning the cultural and ideological spectrum but united against the common enemies of State, Capital and Empire.

7. The leadership corps of such movements should ideally be hard line revolutionaries with a commitment to radical action and an understanding of the major issues.

8. Aside from a populist-decentralist economic platform, such a movement would assemble coalitions of constituent groups at the local and regional level with grievances against the state and in favor of the decentralization of power.

9. Such a movement would seek to establish alternative infrastructure so as to reduce dependency on state services and to transfer responsibility to non-state services following the demise of the state.

10. Such a movement would recognize the legitimacy of armed self-defense against the ruling class, and so seek to establish private defense forces independently of the state.

So what would the endgame be?

1. Limited, decentralized and federative political institutions and the elimination of the gargantuan states of modernity.

2. Cooperative, decentralist economics outside the modern fiefdoms of State-Capitalism.

3. Non-interventionist foreign policy in opposition to both neoconservative global democratic revolution and leftist human rights internationalism.

4. Defense of civil liberties and individual freedom across the board, whether on seemingly right-wing populist issues like the right to bear arms or seemingly left-wing counterculture issues like drug decriminalization.

5. An authentically pluralist approach to social and cultural matters, where the basis of social organization is autonomous ethnic, religious, cultural, familial, linguistic, sexual, commercial, aesthetic or other such particularist enclaves.

So how do we get started?

To some degree, we see the beginnings of such a movement in the Ron Paul campaign, a grassroots revolt against the neocons' foreign policy agenda, Kirkpatrick Sale's and Michael Hill's alliance of neo-secessionist factions, the emergence of the New Right as a genuine intellectual challenge to Liberalism and Marxism, the resolutions local communities have issued against the Iraq war, the Patriot Act and other abominations of the present system, the success of popular referendums in favor of medical marijuana, the rise of the militia movement in defense of the 2nd Amendment in the 1990s, the rise of the anti-globalization movement a few years later, the economic scholarship advanced by Kevin Carson and other contemporary decentralists, and many other things that serve as prototypes for what might be done in the future. I favor a trickle-down/trickle-up, inside/outside strategy. This means at the top level we need a new generation of scholars to emerge that challenge the hegemony of neo-conservatism and reactionary leftism in the cultural and intellectual realms. At the bottom level, we need street fighting radical activists devoted to the kinds of ideas that have thus far been outlined. We need those who work on the outside (like citizens militias confronting agents of the state when necessary or feasible) and on the inside (lawyers and lobbyists fighting the system on its own turf like the ACLU or the NRA).

Obviously, there is much work to be done.

Organizing the Urban Lumpenproletariat

For some time now, I have argued for an alliance of left-wing anarchism and right-wing populism against the common enemies of imperialism and Big Brother statism. I have argued that the strategic application of such an alliance would be a pan-secessionist movement rooted in the traditions of the American Revolution and the later Southern War of Independence. Secessionism is often associated with political conservatism, given the greater regard of conservatives for American traditions like states' rights and the conservative nature of the Southern secession of 1861. Indeed, pro-secessionist rumblings have emerged in the mainstream Right recently. Such developments are a welcome thing, of course, and no doubt a future pan-secessionist movement would have a strong right-wing and radical center constituency behind it. As the middle class continues to sink into the ranks of the underclass, and as the vast array of cultural groups associated with right-wing populism continue to come under attack by the forces of political correctness, no doubt an increasing number of people, including many former jingoists, members of the religious right and one-time neocon sympathizers, will realize that the centralized liberal-managerial regime is their enemy, and decide that a political exodus is their best bet. Certainly, a mass army of secessionists in the rural areas, small towns and red states will be a welcome addition to our cause.

However, I do not think that it is on the Right that the crucial political battles will be fought. The Right represents an agglomeration of political, cultural and demographic factions that are losing power and shrinking in size. Instead, the crucial battles will be fought on the Left. The dominant center-left that is now consolidating its position is a liberal Left that espouses liberal internationalism, universalism, humanism and human rights imperialism, and expresses itself in the form of the therapeutic-managerial-welfare state. However, there is an emerging radical Left that is oriented towards pluralism, postmodernism, cultural relativism, pro-Third Worldism and anti-Zionism. Eventually, there will be a sharp split between these two lefts, as the former is capable of cooptation by state-capitalism, but the latter is not.

Can a radical Left that is fervently anti-Israel and pro-Third World nationalism ever be reconciled with the American ruling class? It is highly unlikely. Furthermore, the spectacle of conservative Muslims, feminists, gays, transgenders, Marxists, anarchists, leftists, nationalists, national-anarchists, Jews, anti-Semites, racialists, anti-racists, peaceniks and Hamas sympathizers marching against Zionism and U.S. imperialism is not only a potential ruling class nightmare, but a manifestation of the kind of pluralistic, culturally relativist, cross-ideological alliances against the System that I have been arguing for in the past.

The legitimizing ideological superstructure of the present regime and ruling class, i.e., liberalism, is antithetical to both paleoconservatism from the Right and cultural relativism from the Left, but there is sufficient enough overlap between these latter two as to make strategic alliances possible. We see the beginnings of this in the current alliance between bioregionalist and Green decentralist left-wing secessionists and conservative Christian right-wing secessionists. As left-liberalism continues to become an increasingly status quo and upper middle class ideology, the radical Left will find itself increasingly alienated from liberalism. The more deeply entrenched political correctness becomes, the more it will alienate even many of its former sympathizers.

The real political war of the future will be between not only the liberal-left and the postmodern left, but between the totalitarian and anarchistic left, and the New Class and the underclass. Just as the U.S. Civil War sometimes found members of the same family on different sides of the fence, so will the future political war find members of constituent groups from the contemporary Right and contemporary Left on both sides. If the battle is between liberal universalism and relativist pluralism at the intellectual level, then the natural political expression of the latter would be some kind of decentralized anarcho-pluralism, with its popular form resembling something like left-conservatism or pan-secessionism.

Although most of the actual secessionist movements at present are rooted in the red states or the more maverick blue states like Vermont and New Hampshire, a serious pan-secessionist movement will need to be first and foremost oriented towards the large metropolitan areas. This is where the majority of the U.S. population resides. It is where the plutocratic elites, state bureaucracies and New Class managerialists are located, and it is also where the lumpenproletarian masses are located. The large cities are where the paramilitary police forces are located and they are where most of the residents of the prison-industrial complex originate from.

The goal of a serious pan-secessionist movement whose aim is to overthrow the empire for real should be to obtain political preeminence in large cities as a first order of business. Cities tend to be dominated by the aforementioned plutocratic elites, and by landlords, developers, and well-heeled civic and business interests. These elements are for the most part bought into the System, and can therefore never be converted to our side. So strategically speaking, an urban secessionist strategy will generally have the flavor of plutocratic/bureaucratic elites vs. Everyone Else. Recognition of this fact implies the necessity of a class-based radical movement rooted in the lumpenproletariat, petite bourgeoisie, lower respectable poor, lower middle class, bohemians and déclassé elements. The goal is to obtain a political majority capable of seizing power at the municipal level in large metro areas. Once political preeminence was obtained in a fair number of cities, a formal alliance of municipal secessionist movements could be formed, and these could form a wider alliance with secessionists among the Red Staters, Greens, indigenous people and so forth. In "Liberty and Populism" I wrote:

> We need to abandon the bourgeoisie identity politics that have grown out of the New Left. The legacy of this has been to create a constituency for the left-wing of capital among elite members of traditional minority groups including educated professionals among blacks, feminists and homosexuals, middle-class ecology enthusiasts and animal-lovers and so on. The best approach here would be to attempt to pull the rank-and-file elements of the traditional minorities out from under their bourgeoisie leadership. This means that anarchist revolutionaries such as ourselves would need to seek out common ground with nationalist and separatist elements among the non-white ethnic groups against the black bourgeoisie of the NAACP, poor and working class women against the upper-middle class feminist groups like NOW and the gay counter-culture (complete with its transsexual, hermaphrodite and "transgendered" elements) against the more establishment-friendly gay middle-class.

Indeed, we have not even begun to touch on the possibilities for building a radical movement rooted in part in marginalized social groups ignored, despised or persecuted by the establishment. These elements include the handicapped, the mentally ill, students, youth, prostitutes and other sex workers, prisoners, prisoner's rights activists, advocates for the rights of the criminally accused, the homeless and homeless activists, anti-police activists, advocates of alternative medicine, drug users, the families of drug war prisoners, immigrants, lumpen economic elements (jitney cab drivers, peddlers, street vendors), gang members and many others too numerous to name. On these and other similar issues, our positions should be to the left of the

ACLU. Adopting this approach will bring with it the opportunity to politically penetrate the rather large lumpenproletarian class that exists in the US with little or no political representation. At the same time, the last thing we should wish to do is emulate the mistakes of the new left by adopting an ideology of victimology and positioning ourselves as antagonists of the broader working masses. Nothing could be more self-defeating. The defense of marginal population groups in a way beyond any efforts in this area offered by the left establishment should be part of our program, but only part. Our main focus should be on the working class itself, the kinds of folks who work in the vast array of service industries that comprise the bulk of the US economy.

There are several reasons for these positions. The first is rooted in recognition that as the Left has abandoned class-based politics in favor of the cultural politics of the left-wing of the upper middle class. It is only natural that we should step in to fill the void. The second is rooted in recognition of a wide assortment of out groups that have never made it into the Left's pantheon of the oppressed/victimological coalition, and the possibility of recruiting from these groups in order to increase our own numbers. The third is to undermine liberalism's claimed monopoly on do-gooderism. A pan-secessionist movement that is seen as the simultaneous champion of the ordinary working poor and the marginalized and persecuted such as the homeless, punk rock squatter kids, mental patients, drug addicts, prisoners, et.al. Such an approach will much more easily deflect the charges of "fascism and racism" that will be thrown in our direction. The fourth is to undermine liberalism by splintering its constituent groups.

Note that I am not implying anything politically correct here. For instance, while we might uphold the legitimate rights of gay organizations, businesses or individuals that come under attack by the state, and practice non-discrimination within the context of our own alternative infrastructure radical organizations, this does not mean that we will allow "gay rights" organizations allied with the liberal enemy to dictate who can or cannot be a part of our own movement. Being a primarily lower class movement, it is only natural that many people with conservative views on sex, morality, religion and the like will also be included within our ranks. Likewise, we may support organizational efforts set up to provide genuine assistance to transgendered people (even the Iranians do this), drug addicts, the handicapped, people with AIDS or other special populations, but we do not insist on the universalization of liberalism. For instance, we might also be just as supportive of skinhead squatters as leftist punk rock squatters, national-anarchists as leftist-anarchists, separatist tendencies among redneck white communities along with black separatists. More broadly, the radical movement would vehemently defend all victims of political correctness wherever they can be found just as strongly as we might defend victims of police brutality. We would defend students harassed by school authorities for carrying Bibles or other religious artifacts just as quickly as we would defend students harassed in a similar fashion for wearing "Goth" clothing. While in urban areas at least, we would take a liberal-left-libertarian, ACLU-like approach to cultural and social matters, with some exceptions like our own defense of the right to bear arms, unlike left-liberals we would recognize that controversial social questions like abortion and gay marriage are best handled at the local level according to community standards. While our own worker, tenants, squatter, and prisoner defense organizations would out of necessity be inclusive of both natives and immigrants, even illegal immigrants in some instances, this does not mean we would necessarily accept carte blanche immigration as a matter of principle.

The question of race is a particularly interesting and challenging one. African-American anarchist Mark Gillespie offered this assessment:

> Whether you are a homo-leftist-anarcho-syndicalist-voluntary-eco-feminist or a racist-ultra right-wing-neo-conservative-constitutionalist-patriot, both agree that the State, in its current form, is detrimental to their views

and lifestyles. In this "society", these groups are kept from uniting by the activity of the state and its media. However, we know that in the realm of anarchy diversity of views is strength and not weakness. We have allowed the State to divide us based upon the most trivial things.

The fact is that, under anarchy, all of these different groups may "have it their way". If the an-caps want a completely free market economy for themselves and the an-coms want to combine in communes, they can do this better under anarchy than they can now. If the Homo-an-syn-fem (hell of a moniker, yes?) wants to separate from the Neo-con-con-pat or vice versa, they can and do it more peaceably than they can under statism. This is the best weapon of an anarchist vanguard. We can and should embrace the different elements that make up this country. Think about this. If we can embrace just two major groups under the anarchist banner, we could send the statists home, without a shot.

The major ethnic groups in this country are the New Worlders (Aboriginal Americans, Blacks and Spanish/ Aboriginals) and the Old Worlders (people of mostly European descent). These groups are kept at each other's throats and socially separated by negative media reports and by institutionalized racism. Reports of rampant crime, lack of morals and mob violence send shivers down the spines of the average, patriotic, "law-abiding", traditionalist citizens, amongst the Old Worlders. Historic wrongs, appeals to end needed restorative services in the community and an envy for those who seem to do better than them, keeps New Worlders in the grip of a fear that the statists work hard to instill. Neither one of these groups are necessarily wrong, but, their fears and hatred, spread and protected by the weapons of the state, virtually ensures that these two major groups will meet together, only when they are pointing guns at each other.

The New Worlders make up a combined 25.7 percent of the nation's population (approximately 72 million people). Let's assume that the mostly Old Worlder patriot movement makes up about 3 percent of the white population (approximately 6.5 million). With these numbers, and a properly educated and motivated anarchist vanguard, there are at least 32 different states that are immediately vulnerable to a takeover and disbanding of the state government (based upon a population of less than 5 million/state) and any state in the union is vulnerable to a gradual takeover.

Something like 32 states and maybe 50 major cities sounds about right. I'm also inclined towards the view that an anti-state, pan-secessionist revolutionary movement would actually have a disproportionately high number of racial and ethnic minorities. Of course, even this would not stop our enemies from throwing the "racist and fascist" label in our direction. Of course, the proper response to such accusations would not be persistent denial and attempts at clarification but a simple middle finger. But while we should not treat the politically correct classes with anything but contempt, it does seem natural that a pan-secessionist alliance would indeed include many ethnic sub-tendencies, for instance, blacks in inner-cities, indigenous people in Hawaii, Alaska, the western plains or on reservations, Puerto Ricans *independencias,* Muslim or Arab enclaves in Michigan, Hasidic, Asian neighborhoods in large cities, or Indian Quebecois separatists, majority Aztlan local communities in the Southwest, and perhaps even revolutionary organizations within Mexico itself. Indeed, the pan-secessionist revolutionary organizations might even form tactical alliances with insurgent forces in Central and South American countries or in the Middle East such as Hezbollah or the Farabundo Marti National Liberation Front. After all, it is the empire that is our common enemy. None of this is inconsistent with our insistence on the sovereignty of nations against imperialism, communities against statism, and individuals within the context of freedom of association.

An urban, lumpenproletarian revolutionary movement would be unlike anything that has come before. It would be socially conscious out of the recognition of the economic circumstances of the lower classes and the social conditions of a wide array of marginal population groups. Yet it would shun the political correctness of the liberal upper-middle class and cultural and intellectual elite, and no doubt have a conservative and libertarian as well as progressive dimension to its character.

The Case for a Coalition against Consensual Crimes

Resolved: Opposition to so-called "victimless crimes" or "consensual crimes" has long been a hallmark of libertarian and anarchist thought. It's time the ball started rolling a little bit faster on this question. These kinds of laws are the primary reason why the U.S. police state has grown dramatically in recent decades, and are the primary reason why the U.S. prison population is so large.

While some progress has been made in the areas of medical marijuana and marijuana legalization in recent years, for the most part there has been very little traction on the issue of consensual crimes. This is because neither the Left nor the Right has adopted it as a primary issue in the way that the Right has adopted gun rights and the Left has adopted abortion rights and gay rights. It would appear that this is a natural issue for libertarians and anarchists to take up, and essentially make this into a definitive issue for all enemies of the state.

We need to begin organizing a political coalition of all those impacted negatively by consensual crime laws for the purpose of repealing all of these laws across the board and at every level of government. It would be a mistake to focus on some of these laws on an individual basis (for example, focusing solely on drug legalization or solely on repealing seat belt laws). Rather, it is best that opponents of these laws unite and take up each others' banners in the name of unity of those persecuted by the state. The first order of business might be to make up a list of specific laws to be repealed and policy actions to be pursued. My recommendations would be these:

The Case for a Coalition against Consensual Crimes

- Repeal of all laws criminalizing the possession and/or sale of drugs by and for adults, an end to drug prosecutions and arrests, and the release of all drug war prisoners.

- Repeal of all laws barring consensual adult prostitution, an end to all consensual prostitution prosecutions and arrests, and the release of all prisoners incarcerated for consensual prostitution offenses.

- The same set of recommendations as above with regards to gambling.

- The same set of recommendations as above with regards to the illicit production of alcohol ("moon shining").

- The repeal of all laws pertaining to vagrancy, panhandling, or sleeping in public where this does not involve obstructing traffic, undue harassment, or trespassing on other people's property.

- The repeal of laws barring consensual assisted suicide.

- The repeal of all laws banning smoking on private property if the owner wishes to allow smoking.

- The repeal of all nanny state regulations pertaining to foods, beverages, seat belts, or motorcycle helmets.

- The repeal of all laws barring sexual relationships between consenting adults (to the degree that any of these remain).

- The repeal of all laws barring voluntary, consensual practice of polygamy.

- The repeal of laws criminalizing underage drinking or smoking.

- The repeal of compulsory school attendance laws.

- The repeal of mandatory Selective Service Registration for eighteen year olds.

- The repeal of laws criminalizing or banning alternative food or medical practices such as the use of raw milk or midwifery.

- An end to state harassment of unconventional religious sects.

- An end to the involuntary psychiatric incarceration of persons labeled "mentally ill" but who have not been convicted of a crime.

- An end to mandatory minimum sentencing.

- Dismantling of police SWAT teams.

- Informing jurors of their nullification rights.

This would seem to be a pretty good list to start with. Of course, there is always a gray area when discussing consensual crimes. Some libertarians argue drunk driving is a victimless crime as long as you don't actually hurt anyone. Statutory rape is another gray area issue as it involves people who are not considered adults. Advocating legalizing all sex between consenting adults spills into taboo topics like incest that would make many people uncomfortable. Advocating legalizing polygamy would certainly be controversial, but much less so now that gay marriage is about to be legalized nationwide. There are also those who argue that mere possession of child pornography should not be criminalized. Again, some gray area there. Building an effective coalition of this type may require leaving out a few things that would be the most offensive to the public and to other coalition members.

But all things considered, the creation of a coalition against consensual crimes would seem to be a very practical, viable, and strategically beneficial means of building the leftist and libertarian wings of the pan-secessionist radical alliance and the pan-anarchist struggle against the state.

The Rise of the Grey Tribe

Right now, the most important thing that anarchists, libertarians, anti-state radicals, decentralists, anti-authoritarians, paleos, communitarians, and allied others can be doing is growing the Grey Tribe as a third force in U.S. politics beyond the Red Tribe/Blue Tribe dichotomy.

Growing the Grey Tribe is one of the primary steps that need to be taken towards the application of the ARV-ATS paradigm and strategy (along with continuing to increase popular support for the idea of secession).

The Red Tribe is increasingly being marginalized from the mainstream of U.S. politics, and is instead developing its own regional strongholds, while an emerging Blue Tribe/Grey Tribe conflict is taking place. That fits perfectly with my past predictions as well, i.e. that the Red Tribe would become increasingly irrelevant over time, and that the Blue Tribe would become the de facto norm, with the Grey Tribe emerging as the de facto "real Left" opposition to the totalitarian humanism of the Blue Tribe with the left-libertarian/anarcho-leftoids being caught in the middle. As one writer has stated:

> Everyone knows America has two cultures. Ever since the bitterly contested 2000 Bush v. Gore election we've referred to "Red States" and "Blue States." The states in question of course aren't monolithically "Red" or "Blue" but the color describes the dominant culture of the population of those states. Red and Blue are more clearly thought of as tribes.

The Rise of the Grey Tribe

Scott Alexander describes the American Red & Blue tribes:

> The Red Tribe is most classically typified by conservative political beliefs, strong evangelical religious beliefs, creationism, opposing gay marriage, owning guns, eating steak, drinking Coca-Cola, driving SUVs, watching lots of TV, enjoying American football, getting conspicuously upset about terrorists and commies, marrying early, divorcing early, shouting "USA IS NUMBER ONE!!!", and listening to country music.

> The Blue Tribe is most classically typified by liberal political beliefs, vague agnosticism, supporting gay rights, thinking guns are barbaric, eating arugula, drinking fancy bottled water, driving Priuses, reading lots of books, being highly educated, mocking American football, feeling vaguely like they should like soccer but never really being able to get into it, getting conspicuously upset about sexists and bigots, marrying later, constantly pointing out how much more civilized European countries are than America, and listening to "everything except country".

> The Red Tribe and the Blue Tribe existed long before the 2000 election, of course. In fact these two American tribes pre-date their own nation. They have both existed and been at each other's throats for a thousand years. Their bitter fight has erupted into open mass warfare three (count 'em, 1 2 3) times, and their cultural struggle has never ended.

Scott goes on from describing the Red and Blue tribes to briefly and parenthetically mention a third tribe, the *Grey Tribe*:

> (There is a partly-formed attempt to spin off a Grey Tribe typified by libertarian political beliefs, Dawkins-style atheism, vague annoyance that the question of gay rights even comes up, eating paleo, drinking Soylent, calling in rides on Uber, reading lots of blogs, calling American

football "sportsball", getting conspicuously upset about the War on Drugs and the NSA, and listening to filk – but for our current purposes this is a distraction and they can safely be considered part of the Blue Tribe most of the time)

Partly formed? Someone should do something about that.

The Grey Tribe Is Born

Greys are a libertarian-minded tribe of live-and-let-livers. They tend to dwell online, often adopting shifting pseudonyms and communicating with each other on forums and anonymous imageboards. Amongst the Grey Tribe one would expect to see higher levels of internet savvy, fondness for tech gadgetry, and disillusionment with traditional politics. They support privacy and anonymity, and oppose the NSA surveillance regime. Edward Snowden is a Grey Tribe hero. They revere open source, strongly support an open internet, and it is by no means an exaggeration to describe them as free speech fundamentalists.

Greys tend to have nomadic tech industry jobs. Many are freelancers or entrepreneurs. They engage online and don't congregate geographically as thickly as the other tribes do, except for their noticeable clusters in San Francisco and other technology hubs. They speak in nerd/geek/gamer lingo and signal membership to each other with Internet cultural tropes and catchphrases. All three of the tribes have found a home on the internet but the Grey Tribe is born of the net and has never existed outside of it.

Many of the Grey Tribe self-identify as Blue, agreeing with Blues on many social issues while feeling disagreement with the Blues in areas economic and opposing Blue efforts to enforce political correctness. A few self-identify as Red, strongly agreeing with small government and 2nd amendment rights, but usually feeling strong antipathy or at best ambivalence toward Red social issues like opposition to gay marriage and abortion. Other Greys adopt the libertarian mantle, and many Greys disavow politics entirely. Despite their failure so far to self label as such, the Grey Tribe does exists as its own independent culture, overlapping in areas but remaining distinct from the Red and Blue cultures.

The Grey Tribe has existed as long as the Internet but in the last few decades a generation has grown up on the internet and on its Grey Tribe culture. The numbers of the Grey Tribe have swelled while the cultural and economic power of the Grey Tribe has also risen along with the power and prestige of the tech industry. Grey industries and cultural products have now entered the mainstream and with entry to the mainstream come conflict with existing power centers.

The Grey/Blue Conflict

The emerging Grey Tribe is the result of a schism within the Blue Tribe, who has all but won their long war against the tired & woeful Red Tribe. Greys in many ways are moderate Blues, in that they agree with the general Blue cultural positions on gay marriage and abortion but reject Blue economic and cultural extremism. Many of the technology stories of the recent past are best interpreted as part of a Blue/Grey conflict between Grey freedom of expression and moral values.

Classical Grey libertarianism is assailed as "brutalist" by Blue left-libertarianism. The Grey technology industry is mostly fallen to a Blue insurgency war under the cry of "More women in the industry!" Grey science fiction fandom has been wracked by Blue-instigated civil war. Grey organized Internet atheism has witnessed a breakaway of schismatics in deep Blue Atheism+. And even the apolitical Grey gamers are now under Blue assault.

These varied fights are not separate, they're the multiple fronts of a single large scale tribal culture war that the Blues are currently waging against the Greys for not being Blue enough.

Each of these fronts has simmered independently but of late, especially with regard to GamerGate, the conflict has become so hot that the fronts are bleeding into each other. This war shouldn't be confused with the mainstream Blue vs. Red culture war, which is all but over, this is a brand new culture war by the Blues against a different opponent and it takes place almost entirely on the Internet.

As they become more aware of the larger picture and notice the other fronts, the Greys will begin to see that each of their fights has deeper stakes and is part of the larger important struggle to maintain their Grey culture. The Blues may have overstepped and awakened a sleeping giant. This war may be what results in the Greys flexing their might and explicitly asserting their independence from the Blues.

Could the rise of the Greys be the rise of a new participant in the thousand year war? Will the Reds survive as more than a southern regional culture if that happens? Will the Blues instead succeed at snuffing the Greys out in their crib?

Stay tuned. It's an interesting time to be a witness to history.

Anarchists, Secessionists, and the Grey Tribe: Where We Conflict

In a perfect world, there would be a federation of anarchist organizations, representing many kinds of political and cultural groups with a generally anti-authoritarian orientation (a libertarian Grey Tribe in opposition to the various forces of statism, totalitarianism, imperialism, militarism, corporatism, and fascism). Further, the overarching strategic outlook for the anarchist-Grey Tribe would be pan-secessionism (a kind of contemporary version of the classical anarchist notion of the general strike). It is indeed probable that a relatively unified anti-state force will need to emerge at some point if the enemy is to be effectively combated and overthrown.

However, it is also true that there is also a great deal of division between and among anarchists, libertarians, Grey Tribers, and secessionists. For example, a large majority of anarchists are cultural leftists while a significant percentage of the much larger Grey Tribe is right-wingers or social conservatives. And many serious libertarians, not to mention Grey Tribe sympathizers, are neither anarchists nor secessionists. Likewise, there are many fellow travelers of the Grey Tribe who have a foot in the Red Tribe, Blue Tribe, or some other tribe. How can a coherent much less cohesive movement emerge from such an array of contradictory and often hostile opinions?

It needs to be remembered that we are not yet at the stage where a united revolutionary front is necessary. An effort of this kind may be necessary in the future as the moment approaches when the ruling class desperately seeks to maintain its position and unleashes repression. But that particular stage in the struggle is likely a very good distance into the future.

In the meantime, it is sufficient that different resistance tendencies grow independently of each other even if they remain bitterly opposed to one another in many instances. For example, as anarchist movements grow on a macro-level, many of these will no doubt be very much in conflict with each other on the micro-level. The current rivalries between anarcho-communists and anarcho-capitalists, leftist-anarchists and national-anarchists, anarcho-syndicalists and anarcho-primitivists may actually intensify. So will the conflicts that have been observed between vegetarians and vegans, feminists and the transgendered, anarchist people of color and crustpunks, anarcha-femnists and critics of "call out culture," and many others. However, the pan-anarchist paradigm that ATS aims to advance is primarily concerned with the sum total of the growth of anarchist movements taken as a whole, and not sectarian or issue-based rivalries that may exist between them. As anarchists movements grow to include hundreds of thousands or millions of people, these kinds of antagonisms may only increase, including public brawls and street fights between antifa anarchists and anarcho-nationalists, primitivists and technophiles, vegans and carnivores, feminists and male homosexuals, and many other such divisions.

A similar process may unfold among the wider libertarian-leaning Grey Tribe. There will likely be intense rivalries between thick and thin libertarians, religious and atheist libertarians, left and right libertarians, Red Tribe and Blue Tribe libertarians, racist and anti-racist libertarians, brutalist and humanitarian libertarians, anarchist and minarchist libertarians, pro-life and pro-choice libertarians, and, perhaps most significantly, secessionist and anti-secessionist libertarians.

As secessionist movements grow, there will likely be both anarchists and libertarian Grey Tribers who are opposed to secession for any number of reasons, e.g. contending cultural values, economic questions, foreign policy differences, patriotism, concerns about stability, and other things. There will also likely be rival camps of secessionists who disavow each other, or disavow the libertarians, or disavow the anarchists.

This is not to mention the vast array of single issues (from immigration to capital punishment to legalizing polygamy to religious liberty vs. gay rights) that will prove to be highly controversial as these movements collectively grow.

None of this by itself is particularly problematic from the perspective of the ARV-ATS philosophy, meta-political outlook, or meta-strategy. Our ambition should be to grow all anarchist, libertarian, anti-statist, decentralist, anti-authoritarian, anti-corporatist, anti-capitalist, anti-imperialist and regionalist movements until all of these collectively become a substantial political majority. We should likewise seek to grow our various strategic and tactical concepts such as pan-secessionism, core demographic theory, fourth generation warfare, anarcho-populism, inside/outside strategy, the left-right-center tripartite strategy, pan-anarchist federations, third-party alliances, alternative infrastructure, the 25 point platform, building coalitions of anti-state interest groups, a peoples' economic front, legal defense organizations, civilian defense organizations, identitarian organizations, regionalist movements, and a free nations coalition. We should grow these strategic ideas until a majority of radical and opposition groups are using them.

When the numbers reach this level we will have won by default.

On Building the Revolutionary Party

The Lumpenproletariat as Class Vanguard

On April 27, 2005, Andrew Mickel, a.k.a. Andy McCrae, was sentenced to death for the November 19, 2002 assassination of a Pine Bluff, California police officer in an act of insurrection against the police state and the empire of imperial state-capitalism that pulls its strings. The action in question was a classic "hit and run" guerrilla maneuver, one that Andy may well have learned during his days as a US Army Ranger. Andy was twenty-six years old, a veteran not only of the US Army but of various movements of the Left, including anti-globalization and Palestinian solidarity. He is now at San Quentin on California's death row.

Of course, Andy is the Left's perfect counterpart to Tim McVeigh. The similarities are certainly obvious enough. The question before us involves the relevance of individuals such as these to the struggle to come. Both the United States as a nation and the world as a whole are entering into a new political phase. For the US, the remnants of the Old Republic are rapidly giving way to the peculiarly unique form of fascism represented by the neoconservative/Anglo-Zionist/Straussian cabal that has seized the apparatus of American foreign policy. For the world, the consolidation of a global super state under an international ruling class centered in the Atlantic nations perhaps operating in collusion with their junior partners elsewhere has never been nearer. US Rep. Ron Paul (R-Texas) has pointed out that a motion brought before the United Nations by the US regime would effectively make revolt against any state anywhere on earth into an international crime, to be prosecuted by international courts and enforced by international police and military forces. The enactment of such a provision would essentially be the final building block in the creation of a global government, with each of the previously sovereign nations being reduced to mere provinces within the global super state, with resistance anywhere on earth to any sort of regime being tantamount to an act of treason against the global super state. Of course, the global super state would in reality be a mere front for the US regime and the senior partners in its global empire (England and Israel), now having achieved complete world domination, and pursuing revolutionaries everywhere as part of its generic misnomer, the "war on terrorism".

It is a certainty that if the US continues its current program of imperial aggression and global warfare under the cover of the ideology of revolutionary democratism, the revival of military conscription within the domestic United States will be a necessity. This will in turn be quite likely to produce a good deal more of the likes of Tim McVeigh and Andy McCrae, angry young men with military experience who turn their guns on the System. This phenomenon will also be fueled by the drastic rise in recent decades of persons prone to lethal violence of either a random or retaliatory nature (school shooters, "road rage", "disgruntled postal workers", etc.). Thus far, such incidents have mostly occurred independently of one another and have been directed towards random or personalized targets. However, rising political discontent fueled by an unpopular war (or series of wars), economic decline, increased repression, and an increasingly alienated and frustrated population of youth and military veterans will likely trigger not only an increase in incidents such as the aforementioned but also the carrying out of such actions in ways that are more organized and with more specific political objectives. In other words, as the US continues to degenerate politically, economically and culturally to Third World levels, resistance efforts in the US will begin to mirror those of the Third World, i.e., overt armed struggle.

It is highly significant that those who have taken up arms against the state in recent years have originated from both the Left and Right, often involving similar if not identical issues, particularly police repression. The next phase in the natural evolution of this phenomenon would be a type of political coalescence of the radical Left and radical Right into a new radicalism that defies the old, stereotypical categorizations. Examining the history of radicalism, we see the rise of the industrial bourgeoisie with eighteenth century classical liberalism. The Old Left, with its focus on the industrial proletariat, and the New Left, with its focus on traditional minorities and out groups, have, like the bourgeois before them, becomes a part of the status quo, of the Establishment. The contemporary Left's incessant condemnations of "racism, sexism and homophobia" render impotent the Left's claims of radicalism when minorities occupy high positions among the imperial overlords.

If the vanguard of the new radicalism is not the traditional proletariat, nor the traditional minorities, then who would be? If both the bourgeoisie of classical liberalism and the proletariat of classical socialism have been effectively incorporated into the mainstream of corporate-social democracy, what class then emerges as a revolutionary class? The peasantry, as the Maoists would insist? There is no peasantry in modern societies, though the rural underclass, as will be shown, often comes close. Instead, the obvious class vanguard of the new radicalism becomes the lumpenproletariat, what Marx called the "social scum". We might think of the lumpenproletariat of modern societies as existing on a number of different levels. Several incidents from recent American history illustrate this. During the decade of the 1990s, three major acts of rebellion against the US ruling class transpired. The first of these was the so-called "L.A. Riots" of 1992, involving members of the urban underclass, primarily though certainly not exclusively ethnic minorities. The lumpenproletarian nature of this uprising is further illustrated by the fact that the leadership of the insurrection was often provided by urban street gangs, the closest thing to an actual infrastructure that exists in many urban underclass communities. The second such incident was the militia phenomenon, circa 1994-1998, involving members of the rural underclass, often dispossessed traditional farmers (akin to similarly dispossessed Third World peasants), and composed primarily, though not exclusively, of members of traditional, even reactionary social groupings, including religious fundamentalists, ethnic preservationists, traditional patriots, racialists, cultural conservatives, constitutionalists and populists. The hysterical reaction to the militia movement on the part of the Left establishment, who shuddered at the thought of armed rural ruffians scurrying about, once again illustrates the irreconcilable differences between the liberal cultural elite and the lumpenproletarian underclass. Indeed, much liberal hysteria over private firearms stems from an unarticulated fear of urban minorities among affluent liberals who wear their phony egalitarian credentials on their sleeves.

Lastly, we might consider the possibility of nothing less than a suburban lumpenproletariat, composed of student radicals and bohemian, countercultural and rebellious youth of the type who populated the anti-globalization movement that came to prominence during the famed "Battle of Seattle" in 1999. It is these three sectors of the lumpenproletariat, certainly distinctive from one another, drawn from across conventional geographical, cultural, ethnic, religious, ideological or even class boundaries that form the foundation of the new class struggle, the new radicalism to come. The next logical step in the evolution of this new radicalism would be the emergence of intellectual and political leadership within each of these sectors that collectively understands the necessity of combined efforts among the various subsets of the lumpenproletariat against the common class enemy, i.e., state-capitalism. The primary divisions among the lumpenproletarian class are cultural in nature. This necessitates an authentically multi-cultural approach to the class struggle. Not a monocultural totalitarianism of the type offered by much of the fake "multiculturalism" of the modern Left, but a genuine multiculturalism that actually allows for real and distinct differences in cultural identity, even those that are in conflict with one another. This will necessitate that those in leadership positions be of sufficient caliber as to be able to reach across cultural boundaries for the sake of constructing effective revolutionary coalitions. As militant resistance builds, armed actions against the System will evolve from the level of isolated individuals attacking random targets to the level of organized groupings carrying out authentic military and guerrilla activity within the context of a more coherent strategic agenda. It is the nature of both war and politics that shifting tactical alliances form as new enemies arise. One need only to think of the alliance of the ultra-capitalist United States and the ultra-Marxist Soviet Union or the Aryanist Germans and the decidedly non-Aryan Japanese during the Second World War.

During the early phase of the domestic armed struggle, the insurgent forces will originate on the Right from the ranks of the militiamen, survivalists, common law advocates, sovereigns, neo-secessionists, radical Christian separatists, jural societies, "pro-life terrorists", tax resisters and, of course, the entire umbrella of white supremacists/separatists/nationalists. On the Left, the insurgent forces will originate from among the anarchists, communists, ethnic minority separatist/nationalists, radical environmentalists and "animal rights terrorists". At some point, formal outlaw organizations may also become involved. Joint actions by all of these forces against the common enemy, the System, would put the System on the defensive as the overlords of the New World Order found themselves under attack from all sides, both domestically and internationally. An effective military struggle can serve as a foundation for an effective political struggle. An initial step in this direction might involve a common pact among the insurgent forces to support one another's fugitives and prisoners, regardless of ideology. This would in turn create the foundation for mutual collaboration both inside and outside the state's gulags, and between politicized lumpenproletarian and conventional underworld lumpenproletarian elements.

As the political struggle evolved, newer, less armed struggle-oriented elements would begin to formally join the ranks of the resistance, for example, libertarians and paleoconservatives from the Right or Greens and Socialists from the Left.

Up to this point, the political resistance would largely be limited to issues-prisoner support, resistance to repression, anti-imperialism, etc. However, at some point it would be necessary to create a formal political party drawn from the disparate revolutionary ranks. Several prototypes for this kind of effort exist. From American history, there is the convergence of a number of minor parties to form the Republican Party prior to the US Civil War. From anarchist history, there is the anarchist-led Revolutionary Front of 1930s France, a coalition of radical groups (anarchists, Trotskyites, socialists, cooperativists, unionists) united against both the Fascist and Stalinist enemy. Perhaps the most interesting example of this type from the contemporary world is the National-Bolshevik Party of Russia, which maintains a curious mixture of socialist, nationalist and anarchist ideology and symbolism, but acts largely as an underground opposition party in defense of civil liberty and ethnic minorities against the state, with a strong orientation towards youth.

The battle lines in the international struggle against the New World Order are essentially drawn to pit the forces of state-capitalism and monocultural universalism against the insurgent forces of lumpenproletarianism and multi-cultural, or cross-cultural, particularism. International class solidarity among the lumpenproletariat will require a strategic outlook that is capable of accommodating the immense diversity that exists within the class. The traditional Leftist approach of proclaiming that "the workers have no country" is inadequate, as demonstrated by the way workers rallied to their respective national causes during the First World War, with the working classes of the contending nations pitted against one another on the battlefield. Nor is the contemporary Leftist insistence on glorifying select Official Minorities and denigrating disfavored groups ("straight white Christian males") sufficient. Instead, the ideological superstructure of the lumpenproletarian class must take into account the persistent national, cultural, ethnic and religious loyalties to be found among substantial sectors of our people, as well as the divergence of opinion among our class concerning matters of gender, sexuality, controversial social questions of virtually every type, personal lifestyle interests and so on.

On the national question, the most effective ideological framework would likely be to proclaim individual nations to be in revolt against the imperial system of the New World Order, a type of national revolutionism. This should by no means be confused with old-fashioned nationalism of the conservative variety, which typically tends toward chauvinism and glorification of the state. Instead, the new radicals should emphasize solidarity with other nations in the common struggle against the common enemy. Also, the states and ruling classes within each nation should be denounced as traitors to their respective countries and national causes. While the new revolutionaries would depict themselves as patriots defending their countries against the imperial overlords, they would simultaneously attack their respective governments and state-capitalist elites for their lack of patriotic virtue. This should be done in such a way as to appeal to the traditional culture, history, myths and symbolism of each respective nation. Within this theoretical amalgam, the struggle for the nation simultaneously becomes a war against the state and the corporate classes. Within each nation, the New World Order is met with opposition from both the far Left and the far Right. The next logical step would be the creation of tactical alliances between the two for the purpose of attacking the common enemy, the center-left and center-right NWO elites. Eventually, the far Left/far Right coalition will be joined by the radical Center, the alienated masses likely to be attracted to populist-nationalist, libertarian-socialist rhetoric and programmatic paradigms generated by the revolutionaries. The cultural differences between the far Left and far Right can be worked around through implementation of a cease-fire concerning these matters, and the subsequent development of institutional systems capable of accommodating everyone's interests to some degree. Such arrangements would naturally involve prioritizing the venerable traditional anarchist and libertarian ideals of decentralism, federalism, voluntarism and mutualism. For example, on the immensely controversial question of immigration, authority on this matter could be devolved to the provincial, regional or community level, with "left-wing" communities allowed unlimited immigration and "right-wing" communities allowing zero immigration. A similar approach could be adopted on the matters of abortion, gun laws, drug laws, the welfare state, "gay marriage" and many other things.

Each particular nation usually contains within itself numerous, distinctive regions and localities, each with their own myths, histories and cultural identities. A decentralized organizational structure for the revolutionary party would allow the revolutionaries in each particular community to best utilize the cultural flavor of that community, in addition to creating the means to achieve harmony among otherwise incompatible cultural elements within the lumpenproletarian class and within the context of the broader populist revolutionary struggle that transcends class boundaries. Indeed, the classical anarchist labor movement of the pre-World War One era was often organized in such a way, with distinctive American anarchist groups often existing for Germans, Italians, Jews, and other ethnic populations. How might a similar approach be adopted for the modern revolutionary struggle? First, anarchists need to abandon their current positioning of themselves as simply another branch of reactionary liberalism. It is not enough to simply denounce "racism, sexism and homophobia", pollution and animal cruelty. To do this, we can join the Democratic Party. Instead, anarchists must position themselves as the intellectual and activist vanguard of the New Radicalism, the ubermenschen, or aristocratic cultural elite of the insurgency. The present day cultural elite remains deeply attached to reactionary liberalism, and has therefore expired its historical utility. Consequently, it is time to give them the boot. Instead, the function of the anarchists as the revolutionary vanguard of the New Radicalism is to pull together the disparate elements of the lumpenproletarian class and to "whip into shape" the broader array of resistance forces on an international scale.

Initially, the natural allies of the anarchists are the various separatist movements of either a territorial, cultural, ethnic or religious nature, each of whom seeks independence and sovereignty from the existing nation-state. Within the United States and its immediate territories, these include independence movements in New England, Texas, California, Alaska, Hawaii, Puerto Rico, the former Confederate states, Vermont and others, along with various local independence movements among cities and towns, ethnic separatists such as the Nation of Islam, Aztlan Nation and Christian Identity, religious separatists such as the Christian Exodus movement and the Christian Jural Societies, cultural or ideological separatists like the Green Panthers or Free State Project, and on and on. A positive working relationship between the anarchists and the leadership of each of these tendencies would be the first step toward the realization of a political coalition against the common ruling class enemy. We might think of the structure of such a movement as a pyramid where anarchists are at the top as the intellectual and activist vanguard, operating as "mediating coordinators" of a broader radical coalition of disparate anti-System elements. It would then be the function of each of the separatist tendencies to rally their own rank and file in the common struggle. Particularly advantageous would be the respect commanded by the various ethnic leaders among overtly lumpenproletarian elements, such as street gangs, prison gangs, and motorcycle clubs and so on. Indeed, it was elements of this type that were often among the earliest recruits into the revolutionary militia tendencies of the 1960s, such as the Black Panthers, Brown Berets, Young Lords and others.

Once such a radical coalition was firmly established, the next step would be entry into a larger organization with the aim of conquest of its leadership. The best targets would be one or more of the larger "minor" parties. For example, a simultaneous colonization effort of the Green, Constitution, Socialist and Libertarian parties by proponents of the New Radicalism, and the resulting conversion of each of these parties into vehicles for the new radicals, would create the opportunity for a federation of dissident parties combining the internal resources of each. From this point, numerous constituent groups could be cultivated, everything from homeschoolers and firearms enthusiasts on the Right to advocates of medical marijuana on the Left. A decentralized infrastructure for the Revolutionary Party would allow party activists to orient their propaganda and recruiting efforts towards their respective local cultures. In "red" areas, the New Radicalism might adopt the accoutrements of right-wing populism and in "blue" areas, the adornment of left-wing populism. The inner circle of activists and revolutionary leaders would coordinate their activities on a national scale, but with each group of these focused on their own respective communities. Many anarchists will no doubt look askance at the idea of a formal party formation. However, I believe this approach is necessary given the nature of modern states. At the time of the classical anarchist movement, most states were monarchies rather than democracies, with only America, Switzerland, France and, partially, England and Holland, falling into the latter category. While I agree with critics of mass democracy on the question of this type of regime's proclivities toward tyranny, it is also true that electoral action is of a somewhat greater, if still limited, viability in the present era. Therefore, the Revolutionary Party should be comprised of a political as well as military and economic arm, with the principle aim of electoral action being the election of secessionist regimes to local and regional offices, with these in turn reflecting local cultures.

The foremost ideological obstacle to such an effort is the orientation of much of the conventional Left and Right alike towards ideological universalism, the idea that one particular political, cultural or philosophical system must prevail on universal scale. Much of this can no doubt be overcome on the Right, given the Right's traditional provincialism, parochialism and nativism. However, the utopian-egalitarian-humanist universalism of the Left is more problematical. I am consistently amazed at the number of leftoids who dismiss my own position as "fascist" even though, in all of my published writings, I am persistently anti-statist, anti-totalitarian, and anti-imperialist, reject racial supremacist ideologies and consistently defend pluralism and decentralism. Yet much of the Left, including its so-called "anarchist" wing, persists in hurling the "fascist" epithet in my direction. I can only conclude that the mainstream of the Left, including the "anarchist" contingent, are simply totalitarians intent on erecting an authoritarian cultural Marxist state. We would do well to guard against these in the future.

I predict that at some point in the future there will be a major split on the Left between the egalitarian-humanist-universalist wing and the radical post-modernist/radical multicultural/cultural relativist/overtly Third Worldist wing, as these two are obviously incompatible with one another. For example, it makes little sense to demand the universalization of left-wing cultural values like secularism and feminism while championing overtly patriarchal, typically religious Third World or ethnic minority cultures. Most likely, the cultural universalists will eventually join the Establishment, as their ideology is not fundamentally different from the revolutionary global democratism of the neoconservatives. In the US, the cultural Marxist-neocon alliance, currently symbolized by the likes of Christopher Hitchens, will come about through the neocons' granting the cultural Marxists everything they want in the social realm (expanded affirmative action, the continued legality of late-term abortion, same-sex marriage) in exchange for the Left's signing on to the neocons' foreign policy agenda, a not-too-difficult marriage, really. Meanwhile, the cultural relativist Left may well drift towards the "beyond left and right" camp and eventually find they have much in common with the Third Position, European New Right, national-anarchists, etc.

On Building the Revolutionary Party

In analyzing what went wrong with the modern Left, we have to look as far back as World War One. Previous waves of radicalism, such as classical liberalism or classical socialism, were class-based, with classical liberalism oriented towards the industrial bourgeoisie and classical socialism oriented towards the industrial proletariat. During "The Great War", the abandonment of the international class struggle by the working classes in favor of their respective nations threw Marxist theory into turmoil. Out of this came two new tendencies. One was Fascism, which shifted the focus from one's class to one's nation as the focus of the struggle against international capital. The other was the intellectual ancestor of the New Left, the cultural Marxism of the Frankfurt School, which argued that radicals must first capture the cultural institutions as a prelude to Socialist revolution, so as to inculcate workers with the proper level of revolutionary consciousness. Hence, the Left's shift in focus from the working class to racial minorities, feminists, homosexuals and other groups viewed as potential allies against mainstream culture. A leading theorist of the Frankfurt School, Herbert Marcuse, was the intellectual godfather of the student rebellions of the late 1960s, which largely mark the beginnings of the contemporary identitarian Left as an actual movement. Additionally, two other factors come into play when tracing the roots of the modern Left. One was the failure of Communism and Socialism to produce an egalitarian utopia of unlimited liberty and abundance. While early Socialists like Fourier fantasized about a world where lemonade would run in rivers, real-world socialism, even in its Western non-Communist form, produced little more than a new managerial bureaucracy of the type described by Max Nomad, Lawrence Dennis, James Burnham, George Orwell and others. As a result, the New Left drifted away from proletarianism towards vaguer ideas like "participatory democracy."

The last factor involved in the Left's drift away from class-based politics was the backlash against Fascism and National Socialism, and the racialist or nationalist content of these. The Holocaust no doubt had a traumatizing effect on the mostly Jewish leaders of the New Left. Additionally, the racial upheavals in the US during the 1960s, and the ongoing conflict between the US and Third World "people of color" in Vietnam and elsewhere, provided additional ingredients to a new ideological stew that amounted to a full abandonment by the Left of class struggle in favor of a type of racial/cultural revolutionism that in many ways was the mirror image of the classical Fascism that it was a reaction against. Nothing could be more destructive of class struggle itself. What have been the fruits of the New Left's embrace of identity politics? The cooptation of the bourgeoisie elements within these factions by the corporate establishment against labor and the poor and the emergence of pro-abortion, pro-gay, pro-affirmative action corporate politicians like Bill Clinton, Albert Gore and John Kerry as the alleged leadership of the "Left." In other words, the identitarian Left has actually been a subversive force within the class struggle, playing right into the "divide and conquer" strategy of the bourgeoisie. In recent years, there has been some realization of this on the Left, as evidenced by Howard Dean's pathetic remarks about "God, Guns and Gays" dominating the politics of the white working class in the South, and the analysis put forth by Thomas Frank's recent work. Predictably, the minority of the Left that is aware of this problem responds by condescendingly insisting that the full body of the working class simply become good cultural Leftists. However, a better approach is simply the re-establishment of a class-based radicalism, focused on the lumpenproletariat as the new ascendant class, organized in such a way as to accommodate the wide cultural diversity within the class. Indeed, the emergence of such a movement would expose the Left establishment for what it is, a new brand of totalitarianism, and in the process push the vested interests of the US ruling class closer together.

One can only imagine what the reaction of the bourgeois academics, social service bureaucrats, litigation attorneys, liberal politicians, professional "anti-hate" charlatans and other sordid riff-raff who comprises the Left establishment would be if an authentically revolutionary movement was to emerge. This would be a radical, revolutionary party that favored boycotting federal elections. It would be a party that focused on organizing separatist movements at the local level. It would be a party that was decentralized in its internal structures, allowing for a left-populist approach in some communities, a right-populist approach in others, and an overtly libertarian approach in still others. Such a party could reflect the values of the contemporary Constitution Party in "red" areas and the contemporary Green Party in "blue" areas.

A party that maintained a private confederation of militia, paramilitary and guerrilla forces drawn from the ranks of street gangs, ex-convicts and ethnic minority nationalists in the cities, militiamen, survivalists and disaffected veterans in the rural areas and heartlands, and rebellious or disaffected youth in the suburbs, high schools and universities (perhaps modeled on something like Mao's Red Guards). Left-liberal hypocrites would be shitting in their pants if such a phenomenon emerged. Call it the new radicalism, anarcho-populism, third-positionism, national-anarchism, paleo-anarchism or neo-classical anarchism, whatever you will, such an insurgency would mark the greatest moments in class struggle since the Spanish anarcho-syndicalist uprising of 1936 and the most dramatic event in US history since the Union / Confederacy showdown of 1861. Ironically, we would be utilizing the methods of the early Republicans, formation of an alliance of minor parties for the sake of a revolutionary ideological outlook, in order to achieve objectives similar to those of the Confederates: decentralization and local sovereignty in the face of creeping statism and imperialism. Can the regime be defeated? Of course it can. If the regime can be defeated in the mountains of Afghanistan, it can be defeated in the Ozark Mountains. If the regime can be defeated in the streets of Baghdad, it can be defeated in the streets of New York and Los Angeles. Let's do it!

Building the Pan-Secessionist Meta-Party

In the essay, "Liberty and Populism: Building an Effective Resistance Movement for North America," written in 2006, I made the following observation:

> *Ultimately, we may at some point be able to combine the Green, Libertarian, Populist, Constitution, Natural Law and other minor parties into a single party,... I would suggest calling such a party the "Federalist Party" for several reasons. First, there is precedent for this from American history. Second, it accurately describes what the internal structure of the party should be. Third, it provides a model for the general types of institutional arrangements we should seek to develop. Perhaps our party flag could be an anarchist black flag with the snake from the "don't tread on me" Gadsen battle flag embroidered on it.*

It is now time to begin the application of the core strategic ideas outlined in such ARV-ATS documents and "Liberty and Populism" and "Philosophical Anarchism and the Death of Empire."

Since the above was written, at least two proposals have been put forward concerning how the type of meta-party described above might be organized and what its orientation might be. The most elaborate plan of this kind has been advanced by Ryan Faulk's All Nations Party. The ANP is a proposed pan-secessionist party that would have ethnic separatism as its primary, though not necessarily exclusive, orientation. Another such proposal is Joe Kopsick's Pananarchist Party USA, which seeks to advance the concept of non-territorial governments within a general individualist anarchist framework. While both proposals are a commendable efforts to open dialogue and engage in strategic formulation on this question, in both instances there might also be a bit of overreach.

Twenty-five percent of the US population currently expresses at least casual sympathy for the idea of a secessionist movement in their own region or locality. The principle objective for those of us who have embraced the pan-secessionist strategy should at this point be the awakening of this sleeping giant. The question is how to we turn this mass of 80 million passive sympathizers into a mass of active sympathizers? The first thing that should be recognized is that most of these 80 million potential constituents are not adherents of extremist or exotic ideologies. Instead, the bulk of the opinions held by these people are likely to be rather close to the mainstream on most issues.

There is no evidence that there is a sizable constituency for ethnic separatism within any ethnic group. To be sure, there is a tiny but outspoken minority of people within all ethnic groups who advocate for ethnic separatism, but the sum total of all ethnic separatists within all ethnic groups would still be a tiny fraction of the 320 million people who make up the US population. It is also true that there are many people who practice *de facto* ethnic separatism, but this largely reflects the economic and lifestyle choices of individuals, and is a far cry from advocating *de jour* ethnic separatism as a matter of ideology or moral conviction. While it is certainly true that ethnic separatists can also be pan-secessionists, it is unlikely that a pan-secessionist meta-party (PSMP) that advances ethnic separatism as a primary value will win a great deal of sympathy.

Likewise, it is unlikely that a PSMP that is primarily oriented towards the promotion of an esoteric or exotic ideology will gain much of an audience. While there are certainly plenty of historical precedents for such concepts as non-territorial governments, such ideas are also culturally alien to the overwhelming majority of persons in North America. Therefore, it would be unwise to adopt an ideological stance of this kind as principal strategic objective.

However, the concept of secession maintains very powerful roots within mainstream American history, culture, and politics for reasons that are too obvious to require discussion. Further, secession is a tactical concept that can be embraced by movements of any ideological, cultural, ethnic, religious, or economic orientation. How then should a PSMP organize itself?

The All Nations Party idea of a PSMP that functions as an umbrella for a set of constituent parties and regional or local secessionist movements that have their own interests is generally a solid one. However, I would suggest that at the meta-party level the PSMP should have only two stated objectives:

1. Promoting, advocating, legitimizing, and legalizing the right of secession by regions and localities from larger governmental units.

2. Promoting, advocating, legitimizing, and legalizing the right of minor parties to participate in public elections against the present two-party duopoly.

From this basic starting point, the constituent parties and secessionist movements associated with the PSMP would have every right to advocate for whatever philosophies or issues they wished. For example, the PSMP would have no position on foreign policy. If a collection of red state secessionists wished for the red states to go to war with ISIS, then so be it. The PSMP would have no position on economics. Presumably, for example, there would be both advocates of socialism and capitalism within the PSMP. The PSMP would exist only for the purpose of defending the rights of constituent groups to form their own parties or secessionist movements advocating for any ideas that they wished, and to strip away political and legal barriers to both competitions in public elections by minor parties and secession by regionalist movements. This is does not in any way mean that any constituent party, organization, or movement of the PSMP would abandon or even downplay any of its other issues. It simply means that the PSMP would provide an organizational umbrella for the advancement of the interests of all minor parties and secessionist movements at the collective level. Within the framework of the PSMP, socialists would still advocate for single-payer healthcare, libertarians for tax cuts, social conservatives for the pro-life cause, and social leftists for LGBT issues. The PSMP would no doubt include many constituencies who were otherwise antithetical to each other, such as the Prohibition Party and the U.S. Marijuana Party.

In this sense, it must be understood that the PSMP would maintain both macro-level constituencies and micro-level constituencies. At the macro-level, the PSMP would have only two constituencies: the 25% and growing number of Americans who sympathize with the idea of secession, and those who prefer alternatives to the two-party duopoly. At the macro-level, the PSMP would exist only to promote the two issues of third party rights and secessionist rights, and these issues would be promoted in the same way that proponents of marijuana legalization, gay marriage, gun rights, gun control, the right-to-life or abortion rights have promoted their own issues. At the micro-level, the PSMP would have many constituencies, i.e. the constituencies of its component parties, organizations, movements, and the issues raised by each of these. Obviously, the opportunity would arise within such a scenario for an infinite variety of conflicts between the various constituents of the PSMP, and such conflicts are to be expected. Therefore, mutual agreements among the PSMP constituents would have to be formulated in order to maintain the common peace to the greatest degree reasonably possible. The most practical approach would be for the various constituent forces to simply agree to stay out of each other's backyards. For example, the constituents forces that trended rightward would agree to focus their organizing and recruiting activities on the "red" demographic sectors of the US, and the forces that trended leftward would agree orient themselves towards organizing among the "blue" sectors.

At the national level, the presidential candidates of the PSMP would run solely on the two core principles of the PSMP: advocating for the rights of third parties, and the rights of secessionists. Preferably, the presidential ticket would be split between the Left and Right. For example, the presidential candidate might be from the Socialist Party or the Green Party, while the vice-presidential candidate would be from the Libertarian or Constitution Parties. Further, the Left/Right split ticket should be reversed every four years. For example, in the 2016 election (this is being written in early 2015) the presidential candidate might be from the Left with the vice-presidential candidate might be from the Right. In 2020, the presidential candidate would then be from the Right while the vice-presidential candidate would be from the Left.

All other candidates of the PSMP would run on joint tickets of both the PSMP and their respective constituent parties. For example, the candidate for the governorship of Massachusetts might run on the tickets both the PSMP and the Socialist Action Party, and a comparable candidate in Texas might run on the tickets of both the PSMP and the Objectivist Party. Once again, in order to avoid overlap, rival constituent parties and organizations would mutually agree to stay out of each other's backyards. Additionally, the candidates from minor parties and secessionist movements might also be combined at times. For example, a candidate in Georgia might stand simultaneously for the PSMP, Constitution Party and the League of the South, while a candidate in Oregon might stand for the PSMP, Green Party and Cascadia.

An approach of the kind that has been outlined above would serve multiple purposes. One would be to simply awaken the sleeping giant of potential secessionist sympathies among one-quarter of the U.S. population, and to challenge the Democratic-Republican two-party duopoly. Yet another would be to create a forum where many different kinds of people with otherwise opposed philosophies would be able to work with one another against the common enemy. A third would be to create a prototype for the kind of system that might exist following the inevitable demise of the present system, a decentralized system based on the principal of self-determination for all.

Of course, the emergence of a PSMP of the kind described above would also receive a great deal of criticism from a variety of sources. The critics would include ideologues and sectarians of both the left and right, the professional anti-rightist cottage industry, anti-leftists of a comparable nature, avowed statists and totalitarians, neoconservatives, jingoists, the party hacks of the system's parties, their kept media, and, of course, the overlords of the system themselves. So be it. Revolutionaries without enemies are not revolutionaries at all.

Of course, some from the general anarchist milieus will object that party politics is antithetical to the wider anarchist values of rejection of the state. I previously address this question in "Liberty and Populism":

> *Some anarchists will no doubt object that my approach reeks far too much of a reformist/electoralist outlook. While I certainly respect this point of view, I believe it is unnecessarily sectarian and archaic. The classical anarchists often advocated boycotting elections and for good reason. In most of the countries where the classical anarchist movement existed on a scale of any significance, the "right to vote" was either non-existent or the franchise was very limited. Even in nominal democracies like Switzerland and America, women and other large population groups were denied the vote. Even at that, many Spanish villages elected anarchist mayors and village councils in the years leading up to the civil war. I believe modern anarchists need to develop an approach to this question that is relevant to*

the nature of modern states and modern societies. The approach I favor is one of cold realism and pragmatism. It is indeed possible for ordinary people with conventional levels of resources to be elected to local and state offices in many parts of the US. Persons who achieve some level of success in this area are then in a position to influence appointments to other positions of influence. This can be very important as a means of keeping the worst elements away from seats of power.

It should also be pointed out that the PSMP would be merely a means to an end, and not an end unto itself. It would merely be a vehicle for promoting and popularizing a wider subversive agenda. Further, it would create a framework that would allow anarchists to reach out to and connect with people from all over the cultural and political spectrum, and experience the opportunity to work with a vast array of dissidents as equal partners towards common goals. Anarchists would have the opportunity to embed themselves in the PSMP for the purpose of pursuing a more radical line and the advancement of more extraneous issues that are among the unique concerns of anarchists. Just as the myriad of constituent parties and movements of the PSMP would maintain their own objectives, and pursue those objectives within other contexts and anarchists would do the same thing. Specifically, anarchists might concentrate their own efforts on local politics, and strive for the achievement of political preeminence in an increasingly greater number of cities, towns, and counties. Two, three, many Christianias, Marinaledas, Mondragons, and Kobanis could begin to proliferate.

Meanwhile, the prototypes of South Africa's conservative Orania community and Liechtenstein's libertarian monarchical micronation provide models of how Anarchists and the Left might peacefully co-exist with the Right. Further, there might be a parallel pan-anarchist federation that co-exists with the PSMP, and functions as a base of activists and organizers for the PSMP. The relationship between the pan-anarchist federation and the PSMP would be comparable to the relationship between the

FAI, the CNT, and the Anti-Fascist militias during the period of Revolutionary Spain.

The general demographic and electoral base of the PSMP would be that which has previously been outlined in "Liberty and Populism," though periodically modified in order to adapt to changing trends. The PSMP would then emerge as a populist alternative political force perhaps comparable to Italy's Five Star Movement, or the recently formed coalition in Greece between Syriza and the Independent Greeks. There is also the further possibility of the PSMP embedding itself in the major parties on the ground level. For example, Norman Mailer's secessionist "left-conservative" Democratic candidacy for mayor of New York in 1969 is one example, and Larry Kilgore's secessionist conservative Christian Republican candidacy for Senator from Texas in 2008 is another example.

The PSMP and the Pan-Anarchist Movement

Within the context of the PSMP, the pan-anarchist movement would then work to advance its wider body of strategic and political ideas such as core demographic theory, fourth generation warfare, libertarian populism, inside/outside strategy, left/right/center tripartite strategy, alternative infrastructure, cultural organizations that would replace the state's social infrastructure, the 25 point platform, building coalitions of anti-state interest groups, a peoples' economic front, legal defense organizations, civilian defense organizations, expanded cop watch and neighborhood watch programs, tax protests, civil disobedience campaigns, Kevin Carson's "political program for anarchists," Larry Gambone's "populist groundswell" and decentralist economics, a coalition against consensual crimes, a prisoner amnesty movement, a libertarian common law system, a Norwegian approach to criminology, a Swedish or Swiss approach to foreign policy, the city-state system, and much else.

Once again, none of this meta-political or meta-strategic program implies that any of the myriad of anarchist, libertarian, anti-statist, anti-authoritarian, or decentralist factions would abandon their preferred issues. As I wrote in *Philosophical Anarchism and the Death of Empire* concerning the concept of "anarcho-populism":

> Hence, what I am proposing is a new strategic paradigm and, to a certain extent, a new school of anarchist thought that I call "anarcho-populism". This new brand of anarchism would draw on the other schools in various ways. The classical anarchism originally developed by Proudhon would be its foundation. Like anarcho-socialism, anarcho-populism would be anti-capitalist and pro-class struggle. Like anarcho-capitalism, anarcho-populism would endorse property, markets and the independent sector as an antidote to statism, corporatism and welfarism. Along with leftist-anarchists, this new anarchist tendency would support political freedom and cultural self-determination for racial minorities, women, gays and the like but would not seek to mindlessly glorify or privilege these groups or demonize white males. Along with primitivists and eco-anarchists, anarcho-populism would seek to preserve the natural environment, but without the misanthropy and anti-tech hysteria of much modern environmentalism. Like national-anarchists, anarcho-populism would endorse the right of traditional racial, ethnic, religious or cultural groups to self-preservation and political sovereignty and cross-cultural, cross-ideological alliances against the NWO, but would seek to branch out into "mainstream" society rather than seek out reclusive isolation from the modern world.

Presumably, every libertarian faction would continue to focus on its primary areas of concern, from sovereign citizens to anarcha-feminists, and every faction could maintain its own sub-organizational identities within the context of the pan-anarchist federation as well. However, organizing and advancing the PSMP might serve as a common project and rallying point for all libertarian factions.

The main thing that is needed as this point is action. It is necessary for activists to step forward and begin applying the ideas that have been outlined above. How did other movements that have achieved a great deal of success, or at least size and recognition, begin? How did the marijuana legalization movement begin? The movement for gay marriage? The Tea Parties? The anti-Vietnam War movement? The civil rights movement? The religious right? The modern American conservative movement? Surely, there are things that can be learned from each of these.

Anarchism and Conspiracy Populism

Some reflection is needed on what the proper relationship should be between the pan-anarchist movement and the movement(s) commonly labeled as "conspiracy theorists," "truthers," and the like. Technically, the "anti-conspiracy" milieu is not a movement as much as it is a collection of ideas pertaining to a wide variety of themes regarding alleged nefarious plots by shadowy, secretive elites. These theories are highly varied and diverse in nature and include concerns related to such topics as the assassination of John F. Kennedy, UFO sightings, the alleged influence of Satanic cults in elite circles, alternative medicine, fluoride, the alleged death of Paul McCartney, Elvis sightings, the alleged murder of Princess Diana, FDR's alleged foreknowledge of the Pearl Harbor attack, chemtrails, an endless array of supposed "false flags," AIDS, climate change, peak oil, Zionist bankers, subliminal advertising, the alleged moon landing hoax, Area 51, and, of course, the alleged 9-11 cover up. There are many, many other such theories.

However, by far the most important and relevant "conspiracy theory" involves alleged efforts by global elites to create a one-world oligarchic dictatorship under the guise of a "New World Order." The resemblances of this theory to the claims of the left-wing anti-globalization movement are striking. The principle difference is that adherents of the New World Order theory insist that secret societies and shadowy cabals are the primary players among the global power elite, while leftists tend to hold to a more Marxist-like analysis involving multinational corporations, international trade organizations, and the world banking system. However, on the ground level these would seem to be purely abstract, theoretical differences. It is clear enough that both sets of analysis are virulently opposed to the global super class of plutocratic elites whose existence is beyond dispute. Among the ideological factions, leftists prefer to criticize transnational capitalism, libertarians and conservative populists express concern about one-world government, and "conspiracists" are more concerned about secret societies. However, these various interests converge on many issues of practical concern, i.e. the ongoing concentration of power on an international level.

It also undoubtedly true that adherents of various "conspiracy theories" transcend a good many conventional boundaries, including "normal" political ideologies, the boundaries of left and right, ordinary economic philosophies, race, religion, nationality, and positions on controversial issues such as abortion or gay rights. Adherents of conspiracy analysis also demonstrate a much greater sense of urgency and a greater radical zeal than many ordinary rightists and leftists alike, and tend to be disproportionately concentrated among the poor and working class as opposed to the affluent and wealthy. Additionally, the establishment seems to genuinely fear conspiracy theorists in a way they do not when it comes to ordinary leftists and rightists.

The pan-anarchist movement is about uniting anarchists, libertarians, decentralists, anti-authoritarians, anti-statists, oppositional subcultures, adherents of alternative economics, and anti-imperialists against the global power elite in favor of a general paradigm of self-determination for all. To be sure, there are important cultural obstacles to the creation of a such an alliance, which is why I have endeavored to introduce anarchists to the thought of intellectuals such as Alain De Benoist and Alexander Dugin, and their advocacy of a genuine cultural pluralism that accepts the legitimacy of a multiplicity of cultures with a wide divergence concerning their core values.

This is a perspective that seems highly relevant and complementary to the principles of anarchist decentralism even if one rejects some of the other ideas of these thinkers. At present, much of the anarchist milieu holds to a standard brand therapeutic leftism with regards to cultural questions, and those who don't often fall back on a conventional rightist perspective. The incorporation of ideas similar to those of Dugin or Benoist would clearly be an advance in anarchist theory and thought.

However, the question also remains of how to go about generating propaganda, recruiting, and organizing on the ground level. At present, substantial sectors of the anarchist milieu continue to focus principally on various youth cultures, the far Left, and the sexual minority subcultures. Yet an embrace of the conspiracy milieu would seem to be a way to dramatically increase not only the numbers but the diversity of the anarchist camp. Certain stands within anarchism have already begun such an effort.

On an organizational level, it would appear that the best route for anarchists would be to strive for the creation of international federations similar to the old Anarchist and Communist internationals that existed in the early twentieth century and which are inclusive of the many different kinds of anarchism and overlapping ideologies. The different kinds of anarchists would continue organizing and recruiting among their respective cultural milieus, but towards the wider aim of building populist movements on a nation-by-nation, region-by-region, community-by-community basis for the purpose of attacking the global power elite, and decentralizing political and economic power to the level of the natural community. The incorporation of conspiracy analysis into the anarchist strategic paradigm would seem to be a powerful weapon for the cultivation of "grass roots" populist movements that would in turn be among the most significant constituencies for anarchist-led popular organizations, economic enterprises, front-parties, and civic militias.

Everything I Predicted Has More or Less Become True

In the early to middle 2000s I produced a number of documents that I still consider to be the core theoretical foundations of the ATS philosophy and strategy. These documents contained a number of predictions concerning domestic US politics and international relations, so it is interesting to revisit these with the perspective of hindsight.

In "Philosophical Anarchism and the Death of Empire" (2003) I predicted that U.S. unipolar hegemony was a transitional phase that would likely recede and be eclipsed by the emergence of a global super class divided into multipolar factions, and which was increasingly being challenged by populist movements, rogue states, and non-state actors. This appears to be happening at present given the increasing assertiveness of Russia, the rise of the BRICS axis, the Resistance Block, Latin American populism, the ongoing proliferation of terrorist organizations, and the rise of opposition movements from the Left and Right in the core as well as on the periphery. This recent piece by Noam Chomsky, the Left's leading intellectual, recognizes these trends, and I further elaborated on these ideas in a relatively recent speech on how these various forces are presently challenging the hegemony of the Anglo-American-Zionist-Wahhabist axis.

In "Liberty and Populism: Building an Effective Resistance Movement for North America" (2006) I described the ongoing leftward drift of the United States. I elaborated further a few years later in "Is Something Really Wrong with Kansas?" (2009). I did this by providing an analysis of demographic trends and their relationship to voting patterns in U.S. elections. Ten years ago, I offered this assessment of the ideological drift of the U.S. political class and hegemonic intellectual class in response to the achievement of dominance in the Republican Party by the neoconservatives, and the parallel rise of the "cultural Marxists" (what I called totalitarian humanists) as their primary rivals:

> The US ruling class has continually drifted leftward over the last century to the point where the "Old Left", the Marxist/Trotskyite/New Deal intellectual Left of the 1930s, are now the ostensible conservative Republicans while the Marcusean cultural Marxists of the 1960s "New Left" are now the liberal Democrats. If this historical pattern continues, then an on-going leftward drift will mean that within a couple of decades the ostensible "conservatives" or "right-wing" will be the present day reactionary liberalism of Dianne Feinstein, Charles Schumer, Ted Kennedy, Jimmy Carter, Bill and Hillary Clinton, Albert Gore, John Kerry, Michael Moore and Morris Dees. We can easily envision an ideologically and intellectually decrepit lot such as these presiding over the final days of the crumbling US Empire.

In "The New Totalitarianism" (2007), I predicted an eventual convergence of the neoconservatives' foreign policy paradigm, the neoliberal economic paradigm, and the totalitarian humanist social paradigm. This process is now occurring as evidenced by the fact that the Hillary Clinton camp and the neoconservatives are moving closer together in response to the rise of populist movements, represented by Sanders on the Left and Trump on the Right (although one thing I fortunately got wrong was when I predicted the central figure around which this convergence would emerge would be Rudy Giuliani rather than Hillary Clinton).

I have also in the past suggested that as the leftward drift of the U.S. continued, not only would the "right" come to resemble the Clinton/neoconservative hybrid suggested above, but that the "left" would increasingly come to resemble forces that were at the time to the left of the Democratic Party, such as the Green Party, the Democratic Socialists of America, or the academic left. The left-wing insurgency in the Democratic Party by the Sanders movement would seem to indicate that this is now coming to pass. Some polls now show that Sanders would be more likely than Hillary to beat Donald Trump in a general election, and, ironically, he's not even a real Democrat. He's actually to the left of the Democrats (more in the vein of the Greens, DSA, or the SPUSA) and is only running as a Democrat for convenience.

I have previously predicted that as the right-wing of domestic U.S. politics continues to lose power due to demographic and cultural change, the right would become increasingly militant.

> An authentic Right of the Burke-Metternich-De Maistre variety does not exist in the United States (it never really did) and the closest things to it (the "religious right" and the "white right") represent points of view that were dominant in America long ago but have been losing power consistently for decades upon decades and are trying to "go down fighting". If our principal enemies of the future are going to be the cultural Marxists of the type that now dominate the EU, then we must prepare ourselves for the day when the Clinton-Gore-Kerry crowd is the conservative Republicans. This process is developing very rapidly. The present neocons were to the left of the liberal Democrats of the 1960s. Now they are the establishment Right.

This process is now unfolding as the right-wing of the Republican Party is now coming to more closely resemble the populist-nationalist parties of Europe rather than the older Reagan coalition. I have long argued that the right-wing populist undercurrents in U.S. politics would be a powerful force for some particular movement or leader to tap into, but that right-wing populism alone was not sufficient as a means of achieving actual political power. Instead, I have suggested that an opposition movement in the United States with a right-wing populist base would need to have a crossover appeal to the center and the left in some particular way, such as opposition to neoliberal economic, neoconservative foreign policy, or the excesses of political correctness. As I recently remarked, Donald Trump is now pursuing precisely such a strategy:

> Trump started his campaign with an appeal to the populist right that allowed him to subvert the Republican Party from their right flank and from the bottom up. This was a brilliant strategy on his part and one that allowed him to dislocate the neocons and "movement conservative" shitheads in the mainstream GOP (and good for him!). But now he's moving to the radical center with some Ross Perot-like populist ideas on foreign policy and trade, and he's starting to initiate a crossover appeal the left on class, labor, and bread and butter issues. Again, this is a brilliant tactical move on his part, and one that I always thought would be the winning strategy if the neoliberal/neoconservative paradigm was ever going to be effectively challenged. Recent polls show Trump gaining on Hillary now that he's adopted this strategy... Hillary is now the conservative, Trump is in the center, and Sanders represents the growing popularity of the far left.

In the early 2000s, I also suggested that a range of factors would eventually lead to growing political discontent and the rise of opposition forces of different kinds. These factors included increased disdain for neocon-sponsored wars, widening class divisions, the increased encroachment of totalitarian humanism, the tightening grip of the police state, the increased ineptitude of institutions, and increased cultural conflict due to demographic and generational change. Subsequently, a variety of opposition forces and semi-opposition forces have since emerged. These have included the Tea Party, Occupy Wall Street, the Alternative Right, the Ron Paul/liberty movement, the "truther movement,"

Black Lives Matter, "End the Fed," "Fight for Fifteen," and others.

I have also previously predicted that the more pervasive totalitarian humanism became, the more insane it would likewise become, and this is now occurring in the form of the "social justice warriors" that have emerged online and on university campuses with their fixation on "safe spaces," "trigger warnings," "cultural appropriation," and the like. I also suspected that over time what I call "cracks in the PC coalition" would begin to emerge, and the various factions of the Left would eventually begin to cannibalize each other. The most important division of this kind at present is between the Clinton left-liberals and the Sanders social democrats in the Democratic Party but there are many others that are also emerging or continuing long standing rivalries: Black Lives Matter vs. Sanders Democrats, the transgender movement vs. "TERFs" (a term for "trans-exclusionary feminists"), gay men vs. feminists, vegans vs. vegetarians, "sex positive" feminists vs. anti-porn feminists, Asians vs. blacks vs. Hispanics, etc., etc., etc. Meanwhile, the continued drift of the far Left into the Twilight Zone has produced a huge backlash in the form of the alt right, neo-reactionary, "dark enlightenment," "identitarian," "MRA" and neo-white nationalist tendencies, and many of these tendencies seem to thrive on acting with a vulgar transgressiveness in the face of PC. Additionally, as disdain for mainstream politics and institutions has grown, "conspiracy culture" has also grown exponentially and assumed increasingly bizarre and outlandish forms (such as the "flat earth" movement).

It is also interesting to consider the condition of the various anti-state movements at the present time. Even as cultural, socioeconomic and political polarization are the widest they have been in a century, even as the Red Tribe and the Blue Tribe are faced with what is largely a class based insurgency within their own respective ranks, and even as the Democratic and Republican Parties are internally fracturing, the anti-state movements have achieved very little in the way of progress, with the exception of legalizing marijuana in a handful of states. The Ron Paul movement created a foundation for the growth of the wider liberty movement, an opportunity that was subsequently squandered with almost unbelievable incompetence on the part of Rand Paul. It is now, in 2016, Donald Trump rather than Rand Paul who is the true heir to the Ron Paul legacy (in the sense of cultivating an anti-establishment populism from the right).

Ten years ago, I wrote:

> The crumbling of the US regime within a global framework of greater leanings towards (partial) decentralization and polycentrism will provide libertarian radicals in North America with unprecedented opportunities. It would be a foolish error of a truly historic magnitude if we were to let these opportunities go to waste.

But this is precisely what "libertarian radicals in North America" have done. I suggested at the time that anarchists, libertarians, anti-statists, anti-authoritarians, and decentralists would have to move past their focus on sectarianism, locate common points of unity, and develop a viable common strategy for the achievement of actual political influence. As I said at the time,

> Obviously, the only kind of ideological framework suitable for such an effort would be something akin to Voltairine de Cleyre's "anarchism without adjectives", i.e., a non-sectarian, non-purist, tendency open to anarchists of all hyphenated tendencies as well as their fellow travelers. When I met Abbie Hoffman in 1987, I asked him what he thought the most common mistake made by radical activists was and he quickly replied that the main problem was that too many radicals waste time arguing over secondary issues like this or that "ism" rather than focusing on more immediate problems. We would do well to heed his advice. Larry Gambone describes the problem with doing otherwise:

"Read even the most superficial book on anarchism and you will discover that many forms of anarchism exist-anarchist-communism, individualist-anarchism, anarcho-syndicalism, free-market anarchism, anarcho-feminism and green-anarchism. This division results from people taking their favorite economic system or extrapolating from what they see as the most important social struggle and linking this to anarchism....The hyphenation presents a danger. Like it or not, everyone, without exception, compromises, modifies or softens their beliefs at some point. Where they compromise is what is important. Do they give up on the anarchism of the other aspect? You can be sure that most hyphenated anarchists will prefer to drop the libertarian side of the hyphen. There are plenty examples of this occurring."

In other words, our core creed must be "Anarchy First!" applied within context of decentralism, populism and libertarianism. Here is a set of potential "first principles" for an anarchist-led libertarian-populism:

1) Minimal and decentralized government organized on the basis of community sovereignty and federalism.

2) A worker-based, cooperative economy functioning independently of the state, the corporate infrastructure and central banking.

3) A radically civil libertarian legal system ordered on the basis of individual sovereignty, individual rights and restitutive justice.

4) A neutralist, non-interventionist foreign policy and a military defense system composed of decentralized, voluntary militia confederations.

5) A system of cultural pluralism organized on the basis of voluntary association, civil society, localism, regionalism, decentralism and mutual aid.

6) The achievement of the above through an all-fronts strategy of grassroots local organizing, local electoral action, secession, civil disobedience, militant strikes and boycotts, organized tax resistance, alternative infrastructure and armed struggle.

This is a much generalized program that anti-state radicals of virtually any ideological stripe ought to be able to agree upon. I suspect that those who do not agree might be inclined towards an excess of purism, sectarianism or utopianism.

However, "an excess of purism, sectarianism, or utopianism" continues to be the norm in the various libertarian, anti-state or anarchist milieus much to the detriment of the anti-authoritarians.

There are a couple of issues that are serious obstacles to building an anarchist movement that is capable of a moving past the usual sectarianism that is found among the hyphenated tendencies. Most an-coms and "anarchists of the left" seem to hold to a de facto Marxist outlook on economics, and many an-caps seem to go to the opposite extreme and become Austrian fundamentalists.

The same problem exists with social and cultural questions. Many an-coms (and some left-libertarians) seem to internalize the standard "social justice warrior" paradigm, and anarchists who don't hold to that paradigm often seem to go in the other direction and become neo-reactionaries or something equivalent.

Is it really necessary for anarchists to adopt these kinds of extremist positions?

Is it not preferable to recognize that, yes, the Marxists are right that workers have frequently been oppressed by powerful business interests while, yes, the Austrians are right that state-socialist central planning is awful?

Is it not preferable to recognize that, yes, terrible oppression has historically been inflicted on people of color, women, LGBT people, and others, and that problems still exist in these areas, while recognizing authoritarian dangers associated with PC culture, labeling broad categories of people as "privileged" based on immutable characteristics, the homogenization inherent in global capitalist monoculture, etc.?

As we know, many anarchist discussion forums degenerate into food fights between proponents of these contending views. But perhaps the theoretical premises from which multiple parties are arguing are flawed to begin with?

On the cultural questions, the libertarian writer Elizabeth Nolan Brown offers a potential third way beyond the usual neo-reactionary/social justice warrior dichotomy. However, the economic conflicts are just as problematic.

With the exception of anarcho-communists (who are often viewed by critics as crypto-Bolsheviks), libertarians have an image of merely advocating one step down from state rule to corporate rule, and in the cases of certain kinds of libertarians, it's true. There is a wide range of libertarian, anarchist, classical liberal, an even an-cap philosophies that don't buy into the Ayn Randian "Let them eat cake!" approach to economics, but unfortunately they are the ones with the loudest voices and the greatest public recognition, mostly because they are so co-opt able by the right-wing of capitalism (see the Kochs). The problem with that kind of libertarianism is that there is simply a zero amount of constituency for the repeal of the minimum wage, total deregulation of capitalism, removing all environmental protections, totally dismantling the social safety net, etc. Not 1 in 100 Americans would actually vote for that which is probably the real reason why the Libertarian Party usually gets 1 percent or less in presidential elections. It's ironic that they are so fascinated by markets and yet they never ask themselves why their product is not marketable. They have some good ideas on foreign policy, civil liberties, drug legalization, and monetary reform, but I suspect if any of that is ever implemented it will be done by a left, liberal or conservative party that has borrowed some libertarian ideas. Even the city-states, competing corporate governments, or communes envisioned by anarchists would have to maintain things like social safety nets to ever have any kind of legitimacy. The vulgar libertarian line amounts to "Let's go back to 19th century capitalism!" Clearly, a more well-developed perspective is needed.

The issue of how to attack the international corporate plutocracy is the million dollar question, and this is a primary issue that is just as problematic for an-caps as it is for an-coms. The problem is that it's difficult to fit a serious description of how state-corporate capitalism actually works into a simple slogan like "Taxation is theft." I guess you could say "Corporate welfare is theft" or "Crony capitalism is theft" and that would cover thousands of other things. But clearly we need an approach to economics that will prevent anarchists and anti-statists from being dismissed merely as Marxists or Republicans under another name. There are a wide range of ideas like this already out there but figuring out how to communicate them is the difficult question.

The Presidential Race and the Limitations of Liberal Democracy

This was an assessment I offered of the U.S. presidential contest of 2016 in the middle of that year as the candidates were about to receive the formal nominations of their respective parties (not to be confused with an actual endorsement of any of the candidates).

Some polls now show Sanders actually having a better chance of beating Trump than Clinton. Up until ten years ago, maybe even more recently, it would have impossible for a self-identified socialist to be a viable presidential candidate. I don't think that's the case anymore. The US has taken a huge leap to the left in recent years due to generational, demographic and cultural change, as well as widening class divisions. I think a lot people still don't realize how far left the US has moved. Hillary is actually the most right-wing candidate of the three major ones that are left with her neoliberal economics and her sucking off the neocons on foreign policy. She trends left on social issues, but that's misleading as her constituency there tends to be upper middle class urban cosmopolitan professionals and upwardly mobile members of traditional out groups, and the progressive nanny state her followers tend to champion is the new social conservatism.

Meanwhile, Trump started his campaign with an appeal to the populist right that allowed him to subvert the Republican Party from their right flank and from the bottom up. This was a brilliant strategy on his part and one that allowed him to dislocate the neocons and "movement conservative" shitheads in the mainstream GOP (and good for him!). But now he's moving to the radical center with some Ross Perot-like populist ideas on foreign policy and trade, and he's starting to initiate a crossover appeal the left on class, labor, and bread and butter issues. Again, this is a brilliant tactical move on his part, and one that I always thought would be the winning strategy if the neoliberal/neoconservative paradigm was ever going to be effectively challenged. Recent polls show Trump gaining on Hillary now that he's adopted this strategy. Other polls show Sanders is even more popular that Trump and, ironically, he's not even a real Democrat. He's actually to the left of the Dems (more in the vein of the Greens or the SPUSA) and is only running as a Dem for convenience. Hillary is now the conservative, Trump is in the center, and Sanders represents the growing popularity of the far left.

I don't vote (or at least I haven't since the early 1990s), but there are circumstances where "defensive voting" might be warranted, and even "offensive voting" in some instances. The US state that I live in doesn't usually have referendums, but in places where there are referendums on the ballot regarding important reforms voting might be legitimate. Some states have referendums on drug decriminalization, "criminal justice" reform, and a wide range of issues that might be worth voting for. In some places there are referendums on huge questions, like exiting the EU or Scottish secession from the UK. There are occasionally independent candidates, minor parties, or maverick major party candidates that are worth voting for (the Pirate Party, for example). Sometimes there might also be a party that is so awful that voting against them is warranted so as to ensure their defeat. Who in their right mind would not have voted for the Social Democrats over the Nazis in the 1932 German elections, for example?

At the same time, I do think anarchists need to devote more effort to thoroughly critiquing liberal democracy with its majoritarian-parliamentary-state-capitalist ethos. I think we can also make a distinction between someone like Murray Bookchin's idea of democracy, and the kinds of centralized mass societies under plutocratic rule that we have at present. As an anarchist strategist, I'm in favor of building subversive political parties led by anarchists, or in which anarchists are embedded (like the Pirate Party, LP, Greens, etc) but only as a political arm for a popular movement consisting of anarchist federations that are independent of the state.

We need a multi-pronged "all fronts" approach. Some anarchists will be involved with political parties, some will be forming micro nations like Liberland, some will be colonizing geographical areas like the Free State Project, some will be forming intentional communities, some will be forming worker cooperatives, some will be engaged in direct action like eco-sabotage, some will be doing single issue activism (like Cop Block or Cop Watch), some will be doing alternative media, and some will be involved in direct armed struggle like the Zapatistas or PKK/YPG/YPJ. All of these things are already happening, we just need for them to expand.

One of the most important things to emphasize when we critique democracy is the question of scale. Democracy, socialism, communism, capitalism, etc., all work fine in relatively small, relatively localized groups. It is when these things are centralized into mass society and the state is when the problems develop. For example, there are communists, capitalists, anarchists, theocrats, and nationalists who express admiration for the Amish culture, and to some degree they are all of these things. By the way, the Amish have a great take on voting: "The Amish don't vote in national elections. They vote in local elections. They do so because they have decided long ago that to vote for anyone on the national stage is to vote for a corrupt, lying, scheming Son of Satan. They won't do it. Instead they argue that on the local level their vote just might make a bit of difference."

Crossroads 2016 : Where Do We Go From Here?

As was the case with the previous essay, this piece was written in 2016 during the height of the U.S. presidential election campaigns of that year.

Recently, I wrote about how many of the predictions that I have been making over the past decade or so have come true during the course of recent events. In particular, the 2016 U.S. presidential election represents the fulfillment of some of these predictions. Hillary Clinton is an almost perfect manifestation of the totalitarian humanist convergence I predicted nearly a decade ago, i.e. the combination of militarism, plutocracy, and police statism with ostensibly liberal and progressive values as an ideological cover (with these enforced by means of an ever more intrusive nanny state). Bill Lind describes the implications of this ideological framework very thoroughly. Jack Ross explains the present day political alignments that have emerged because of the rise of totalitarian humanism. And Vanity Fair describes how a new left-wing of the ruling class has emerged that comes from outside the ranks of the traditional WASP elites and is rooted in newer high-tech industries. I've been saying all of these things for years.

Six years ago, I wrote about the ten core demographics that a radical or revolutionary movement in North America would likely need to organize in order to achieve the popular base needed for effective political action. Current events represent the stirring of many of these demographics and in a way that signifies that these cleavages are developing at a much more rapid pace than I thought they would when I wrote that original piece.

The Donald Trump phenomena represents a stirring of the populist right and the sinking middle. The antiwar, civil libertarian, and labor-oriented sections of the Left have become increasingly alienated from both the Democratic Party and the liberal establishment even to the point that some on the antiwar left now favor Donald Trump over Hillary Clinton.

The Black Lives Matter movement represents a movement of black Americans that often demonstrates as much hostility to the liberal and Left establishments as they do to anything on the Right. The Bernie Sanders movement represents the disdain of the progressive Left and the far Left for the centrist-liberalism of the Clintons, and young people in particular seem to be looking for a new political paradigm. A sharp backlash against political correctness has also emerged, and the cleavages among the various constituent groups of liberalism or the Left have likewise become increasingly evident.

Donald Trump's campaign strategy is an interesting variation of the strategy that I outlined in "Liberty and Populism" ten years ago. This involves a strategy of appealing to the populist Right with anti-PC issues, appealing to the radical Center with economic and general anti-establishment issues, appealing to Left with issues that the left establishment ignores or sweeps under the rug, and likewise playing to socioeconomic and demographic cleavages on the Left. Trump is essentially doing this albeit for radically different purposes (getting himself elected President) than those of ARV/ATS (overthrowing the government).

However, it is ironic that during the time that all of this seeming political discontent has emerged, the various movements with an orientation towards anarchism, libertarianism, anti-statism, decentralism or anti-authoritarianism are nowhere to be found. In recent years, there has been some talk about the possibility of secession by various regions of the United States. The left-anarchist writer Kirkpatrick Sale hosted three successive pan-secessionist conventions during the tail end of the George

W. Bush years, and yet nothing ever came of these efforts. There was likewise talk of secession by some on the Right following the re-election of President Obama in 2012, and polls over the last decade have repeatedly indicated that approximately 25% of Americans would be sympathetic to the idea of secession by their own region or locality. And yet no leader or movement has come along that has had the effect of awakening this sleeping giant. Even recent efforts towards the development of a secessionist tendency in Texas have proven to be fruitless. Now that the Brexit movement has achieved success, there are once again secessionist rumblings in Texas. But such efforts have not yet proved to be promising anywhere in the United States to date.

Even the libertarian movement that once seemed to be promising during the Ron Paul moment has largely fizzled. Ron Paul's hybrid of Rothbardian libertarianism and right-wing populism had the effect of developing a wide popular interest in libertarianism, particularly among younger people. However, his heir Rand Paul completely blew it presenting himself as a bland Republican, and attempting to pander to conventional conservatives. If anything, it has been Donald Trump that has been the true heir to Ron Paul's legacy of dissent from the Right. And it is Bernie Sanders that has been the beneficiary of the taste for dissent among younger people that originally emerged during the Ron Paul period.

However, it is also true that the present Libertarian Party candidate Gary Johnson is polling as high as 10% according to some estimates, and the Libertarian ticket may be strengthened by its potential appeal to "Never Trump" voters. The moderate libertarian blogger Scott Alexander has speculated about the possible emergence of a libertarian-oriented "Grey Tribe" in opposition to both the Republicans' "Red Tribe" and the Democrats' "Blue Tribe." Yet it is also true that libertarians have had a very difficult time establishing an independent identity for themselves. This is evidenced by the fact that the libertarian movement that experienced growth during the Ron Paul period has subsequently splintered into a variety of warring camps. Some former Ron Paul supporters have even left libertarianism altogether and joined the neo-reactionary movement.

An additional concern is that, whatever his polling numbers, Gary Johnson and his running mate William Weld are arguably the most milquetoast candidates the Libertarian Party has ever placed on their ticket, as the recent appearance of these gentlemen on CNN indicates.

Clearly, Johnson and Weld are liberal Republicans of the kind that used to be a dime a dozen before the Buckleyite-Neocon-Religious Right takeover of the GOP during the Reagan era. Johnson managed to fumble even on standard libertarian issues like drug legalization during this CNN appearance and Weld, a former federal prosecutor, even denies that he wishes to abolish the IRS. However well these guys end up doing in the polls, their impact will simply be to reestablish a place for old-fashioned liberal Republicanism, and not the development of a revolutionary anti-state movement.

Equally interesting when compared with Johnson's polling numbers is the unusually high polling numbers that the Green Party's Jill Stein is currently receiving. The split that has emerged among Democrats as a result of the Sanders/Clinton contest may drive some Sanders supporters to the Greens. Some polls have placed Stein's numbers as high as seven percent. Both Sanders and Stein represent American liberalism as it was before the rise of Clintonism in the 1990s. Sanders ran as a recycled New Deal Democrat during his campaign, and the Greens are essentially a representation of left-liberalism as it was in the 1970s and 1980s plus some Social Justice Warrior add-ons.

As I have previously written, the most significant aspect of this present presidential election is that the state of American politics is to a large degree returning to what it was in the 1970s, prior to the rise of the so-called "Reagan Revolution," and the subsequent rise of Clintonism as a force which eclipsed both left-liberalism and traditional New Deal Democrats. All of the same factions that were present in American politics during the 1970s now appear to be reclaiming a place for themselves on the national political stage. The principal cause of this seems to be that widening class divisions and demographic change, combined with cultural and generational change, have rendered the Reagan coalition increasingly non-viable, and Clintonian neo-liberalism increasingly unpopular.

Meanwhile, as mentioned above, it seems that a problematic issue faced by anarchists, and others with similar philosophies, is the need to establish an independent identity for ourselves. At present, most people with some kind of anti-state philosophy continue to be largely affiliated with either the Red Tribe or the Blue Tribe, depending on their personal predilections. This need for an independent identity is readily apparent. We should not be merely an appendage to the radical Left (which most people identify with Communism) or the radical Right (which most people identify with fascists and Nazis). Instead, I'm increasingly leaning towards the view that anarchists should position ourselves as the "revolutionary Center" (the people vs. the elite). Right now, radical center ideas seem to be growing in dissident circles.

A good way to frame the issue might be like this: Liberals are the center-left, socialists are the radical Left, and Marxist revolutionaries (like Maoists, radical Trotskyites, and some anarcho-Marxists) are the revolutionary Left. Mainstream conservatives are the center-right, while the alt-right and paleoconservatives are the radical right, and fascists, neo-Nazis, radical survivalists, Tim McVeigh types, etc. are the revolutionary Right. The mainstream center would be so-called "moderates," i.e. centrist politicians with milquetoast versions of some liberal and some conservative ideas. The radical center would be the reformist center with a more populist outlook, and anarchists would be the "revolutionary center," i.e. the centrist alternative for revolutionaries that reject both Fascism and Communism. It is also interesting to speculate on how the upcoming presidential election might impact the future of radical movements.

I'm inclined to think a Hillary presidency will do more to facilitate the growth of authentic anti-system sentiment than a Trump presidency. If Trump loses, more and more people from the Right will think "Well, we tried doing it the system's way, and we lost. It is time for more radical efforts." Meanwhile, a Hillary presidency would inflame the entire spectrum of the right-wing (except the neocons who would probably love her), while simultaneously alienating honest and serious liberals and leftists who would recognize what a vile bitch she actually is, and who would be appalled by the spectacle of PCers and SJWers ignoring her misdeeds as she panders to them. Consequently, many on the Left and Right would start looking for more radical solutions. A Trump presidency would probably motivate the right-wing to rally behind the state under the banner of "Give The Donald a Chance!" and ignore his more negative tendencies. Meanwhile, the Left would be reassured that it's those god-awful "straight white males" who are the real enemy. So strategically, it's probably in our best interests that Hillary win, though that might not be the case from the point of view of actual human interests given the thirst of Hillary and her likely neocon supporters for imperialist war.

Craig Fitzgerald offers an interesting counterpoint on this question:

> I disagree. I see a Hillary presidency as infinitely worse. I actually feel Hillary hates humanity, while Trump does not. I also feel that as long as good populist nationalists, paleocons, constitutionalists & Libertarians don't let their guards down & attempt to influence the Trump camp we may be able to keep him in line. Hillary on the other hand is totally a homicidal maniac.

Gabriel Brown expresses a similar viewpoint:

I may be missing something but it would appear to me that Trump being elected president may actually be the catalyst to accelerate the growth of anti-system politics opposed to Hillary Clinton becoming elected.

Trump is making tall promises that are most likely not promises he can keep 100%. If Trump does not achieve that which his voter base has been promised this could ultimately further crush faith in the system with those on the right who have become fairly moderate in terms of their anti-system position.

This may cause them to move in further direction of radical political positions which will be perfect for our efforts in encouraging them to move beyond the system and beyond the State with alternatives that generally speaking they may not have considered originally.

I say this because I examine Hillary Clinton and suspect that if Hillary Clinton is elected, because she has a manner of neutralizing the population by creating the appearance and perception that business as usual is the way of the system you will continue to see the left lock-step supporting the system and the right ultimately neutralized in actually doing anything radical the way the right is currently not as radical in terms of their efforts with the way the Obama administration has done things. In other words I think that mainstream establishment candidates in power tend to have a neutralizing effect opposed to those who are viewed as non-establishment candidates.

I think people would hold Trump to a higher degree of expectations because he has made claims and promises that do challenge the system whereas with Clinton it is expected she will lie to the public and the public will be neutralized by knowing she will lie to the public.

I could be wrong but it seems to me that Trump may cause people to drive further away from the system showing the public that the system is flawed and even he isn't able to do the job he has promised the people.

Maybe I'm just a closet Leninist but I'm often inclined to make "worse is better" arguments. It is interesting that a lot of the neocons seem to be leaning towards Hillary, and a lot of people from the genuinely anti-imperialist Left are leaning towards Trump (like some of the writers at Counterpunch, Denis Rancourt, Jim Petras, John Pilger, Susan Sarandon, etc). Even Jill Stein seems to view Trump almost favorably when compared to Hillary.

It would seem that what is needed at this point is for a maverick political leader to emerge that is trying to do at the national level what Norman Mailer was trying to do in New York in 1969: Indeed, Adam Kokesh is actually talking about doing something similar to that during the 2020 election.

And ideas of the kind that Attack the System has been talking about for years are increasingly starting to enter the mainstream if only at a snail's pace at present.

While discontent is starting to emerge in various corners, there is at present no revolutionary presence in North America of any immediately identifiable or significantly influential sort. This is one of the first things that need to change. In particular, those of us who identity ourselves as anarchists of some particular type need to begin making our presence known. We need to begin developing common points of unity along with a coherent strategy.

For example, one such ambition might be for genuine revolutionaries to take over these minor parties and turn them into a federation of revolutionary anarchists. The Greens could become the eco-anarchist organization. The Libertarian Party could be the voluntaryist/anarcho-capitalist organization. The Pirate Party could be the crypto-anarchist organization. The Constitution Party could be the right-wing Christian anarchist organization. And the Party of Socialism and Liberation could become the anarcho-communist organization.

The eventual ambition should be to create a national federation of revolutionary anarchist organizations. A principal obstacle to such an effort would be the possible lack of even enough agreement among anarchists about core ideas at this point to hold national conferences or to create a federation of this kind. One problem is that all of these different groups of anarchists (along with scattered individuals) want to abolish the state for entirely different reasons. Some claim the existing state is too capitalist, and others claim it is not capitalist enough. And for some who claim the anarchist label, it's less about the state specifically and more about abolishing capitalism, abolishing violence, abolishing technology, abolishing large-scale production, abolishing patriarchy, abolishing racism, abolishing religion, abolishing transphobia, abolishing globalization or abolishing any number of other things. For all of the hyphenated forms of anarchism, the hyphens usually come before the anarchism. An-caps are capitalists first, an-coms are communists first, anarcho-syndicalists are syndicalists first, anarcha-feminists are feminists first, etc.

I think that the only way around this would be for anarchists and others with libertarian, decentralist, anti-statist, or anti-authoritarian values to develop a common meta-ethic of decentralized pluralism on the macro-level and infinite diversity on the micro-level. Historically, the ideas that comes closest to this are anarchism without adjectives (Voltairine de Cleyre), anarchism without hyphens (Karl Hess), synthesist anarchism (Voline, Sebastian Faure), and panarchism (John Zube). However, this is the main idea I have pushed in anarchist circles for many years and its primary effect has been to make me unpopular with everyone.

Ian Mayes suggests that I am perhaps too pessimistic:

> You seem to have a very sectarian tribalistic view of anarchists, whereas I think that a lot of anarchists are actually not that way. I have met and known a lot of anarchists who are very easy-going as far as ideology is concerned, they claim to belong to no particular anarchist school of thought, or if they do it is a very tepid affiliation with a particular school of thought. A lot of these kinds of people do not even necessarily call themselves "anarchist", they just show up at events that have that label and only call themselves "anarchist" if you really press them on the question. These kinds of people are usually pretty soft-spoken, so you might not know that they are even out there since they tend to keep their opinions to themselves.

Perhaps there is greater reason for optimism than what often appears on the surface. There is also the question of offering a positive vision of what we are for as anarchists as opposed to merely stating what we are against.

While I can only speak for myself, on a general level I am for developing anarchist movements that reclaim the position that anarchists held in the early 20th century as the world's largest revolutionary force before it was eclipsed by Communism. However, I would also like for anarchism to do in the 21st century what Communism did in the 20th century (i.e. overthrow so many governments that they control about 1/3 of the world's nations or more). In particular, I want to see the American empire and its allies taken down, and the next target after that would be the other major nation-states like China, Russia, India, etc. I also wish to overturn the international institutions towards which power is being ceded such as those that facilitate the international financial and trade systems, along with the UN and other similar things. The anti-capitalist struggle (or at least the struggle against corporate capitalism) has to be a core part of this because about 150 corporations control about 40-50% of the world's wealth. All of the various international organizations that have been incorporated into this system need to be overturned (the EU, for example).

There is also the need for self-determination for all regional, national, cultural, ethnic, religious or other groups that are currently under the boot of some external power (Tibet and Palestine are among the most obvious examples). There is a need to attack state repression across the board in all countries and societies. The priorities in this area should obviously vary according to place. Women's rights and religious persecution are the issues in Saudi Arabia, while the wars on drugs, crime, terrorism, etc, and the related police state and prison industry are the priorities in the US. Maybe the excesses of PC would be the priorities in many European nations. There is also the need to develop alternatives to state-capitalism in the economic realm. Ideas of that type have been around for centuries in some instances. I generally think some ideas of that kind would work better than others, though there should be lots of experimentation along regional, national, local, and institutional lines. A big issue in the US is figuring out how to dismantle the military industrial complex. Another thing is to revise law codes along more libertarian lines, along with working to abolish formalized legal systems to the greatest degree possible.

These are just few ideas related to the bigger issues. Many different ideas about alternative social systems are presently in circulation. For example, Wayne Price talks about what a post-capitalist society might look like.

Nexus H. Humectress discusses the need for competing social system:

> Personally, I'd kind of like to see New Hampshire secede and become Ancapistan, bordered by its friendly neighbor, the People's Republic of Vermont, and then we would have a controlled experiment to see which system works better,

a libertarian freed market, or democratic state socialism. My guess is that each of those countries would have its own virtues and drawbacks, perhaps with no clear winner.

Patri Friedman discusses these ideas as well:

Since the EU is basically the opposite of competitive governance (imposing a large, bureaucratic, non-local-adaptive, non-multiple experiments governance structure on a diverse region), I am delighted about Brexit, and hopeful that it demonstrates a first-world trend towards local autonomy and governance diversity. The answers to difficult questions like immigration, security, and foreign policy should not come from a central organization that imposes a uniform solution on all; they should be both locally adaptive and answered in diverse ways so we can all learn from the multiple parallel experiments.

The diversity we need is of the things that matter: rules, ideas, institutions and culture. There should be a country with Germany's immigration policy; and a country with Hungary's immigration policy. There need to be different interest and exchange rates for Greece and Germany. One size fits none. Glad that democracy can occasionally get something right; and psyched for Scottish (scexit? ukexit?) as well as the continuing failure of the Eurozone/ECB to handle widely varied regional economic situations.

There are many single issues that are in need of being addressed. For example, in the past I have expressed what might be considered very far left-wing views on many issues.

On many social questions, I would share ground with... many of the conventionally "left-wing" or left-libertarian positions... I am pro-abortion, pro-euthanasia, anti-death penalty.., pro-drug legalization, pro-gay rights and pro-sex worker rights..., and pro-prison abolition. I'm also pro-homeless, pro-disabled people, and pro-mentally ill, in the sense of favoring abolition of state policies...(such as) loitering and vagrancy laws, zoning and other laws restricting the supply of low-income housing, involuntary civil commitment, regulations restricting the activities of shelters and relief organizations and others too numerous to mention). I am also anti-drinking age, anti-compulsory schooling, anti-censorship and I would put more strident limits on the powers of the police than the ACLU would. I am also interested in anarcho-syndicalist, mutualist, distributist or "libertarian socialist" economics. These positions are well to the left of the Democratic Party, far more left than most liberals and even many hard leftists.

I have also discussed the need for the development of alternative infrastructure and social service organizations.

In terms of offering positive alternatives to the welfare state, I am very much for the development of non-state charities, relief agencies, orphanages, youth hostels, squats, shelters for battered women, the homeless or the mentally ill, self-improvement programs for drug addicts and alcoholics, assistance services for the disabled or the elderly, wildlife and environmental preserves, means of food and drug testing independent of the state bureaucracy, home schools, neighborhood schools, private schools, tenants organizations, mutual banks, credit unions, consumers unions, anarcho-syndicalist labor unions and other worker organizations, cooperatives, communes, collectives, kibbutzim and other alternative models of organizing production. I am in favor of free clinics, alternative medicine, self-diagnostic services, midwifery, the abolition of medical licensure, the repeal of prescription laws and anything else that could potentially reduce the cost of health care for the average person and diminish dependency on the medical-industrial complex and the white coat priesthood. Indeed, I would argue that the eventual success of libertarianism depends to a large degree on the ability of libertarians to develop workable alternatives to both the corporation-dominated economy and the state-dominated welfare and social service system.

However, I am also known for taking a much more accommodating stance towards the right-wing than many anarchists. I've found that, whatever their other views, many from the right-wing are open to decentralization or secession or "situational anarchism" as a practical consideration. I generally lean towards what I call the "Orania solution" for the reactionary right-wing in all its different forms.

I imagine that with pan-anarchism, pan-secession, or pan-decentralization there might be Oranias for white separatists, Christian fundamentalists, Islamists, Catholic traditionalists, Mormons, Zionists, nationalists, social conservatives, black supremacists, La Raza ("The Race"), drug prohibitionists, pro-lifers, homophobes, and all of the other types who reject the central features of liberal modernity just like there might be "Feminazi Towns" with no hookers and porn allowed, or "Trans Towns" and "TERF Towns" or "Vegan Towns" where animals have the right to vote or whatever and "Carnivore Towns." It's just a model for a practical way of accommodating yet containing reactionaries of different kinds as opposed to the totalitarian humanist model of compulsory progressivism or the Stalinist-Maoist-Pol Potist model of massacres.

I also think that it's necessary to have some means of accommodating people who simply reject many of society's prevalent taboos. At present, racism is regarded by many people as the ultimate evil. It may be a backlash against the obvious excesses and atrocities in the past. However, "the racists ye shall always have among you." That may change in the future and something else may come to be regarded as the greatest of all sins. I have seen some evidence that there may be movements to legalize and/or normalize polygamy or incestuous couplings

166

at some point in the future. If so, that will be yet another fight like the gay/trans issues have been, and it will probably cross conventional ideological lines. Of course, let's not forget about the sex offenders, who in many ways are the modern lepers.

The development of something like Federation of Egalitarian Communities or Mondragon or Marinaleda into mass movements is still something else I would like to see happen. I would like to see the international Pirate Parties actually becoming competitive like they are now in Iceland, and I also like micro-national movements like Liberland. "Two, three many Liberlands." We also need more armed insurgent groups like the PKK/YPG or EZLN. It's hard for me to list everything that I'm for because the list is almost endless.

I also suspect these kinds of unconventional political parties like the Pirate Parties or the Five Star Movement in Italy might be the beginning of another trend as the traditional left and right have largely become a spent force and yet certain problems are mounting with no real solutions in sight. Of course, there is a lot that anarchists can learn from various guerrilla movements from the past.

The ideas are already out there. It's just a matter of putting them into practice on a large scale.

National-Anarchism and the American Idea

"Establishing a new world order of supranational government is Hitlerian in concept and will need to be Stalinist in execution."[1]

- Taki Theodoracopulos

"Government is not reason, it is not eloquence - it is force! Like fire, it is a dangerous servant and a fearful master."[2]

- George Washington

"That government is best which governs least."[3]

- Thomas Jefferson

"anarchism ('an-ar-kiz-im) n (1642): a political theory holding all forms of government to be unnecessary and undesirable and advocating a society based on voluntary cooperation and free association of individuals and groups"[4]

- Webster's Dictionary

As long as there has been power and authority, there has been rebellion. From the insurrectionary efforts of Spartacus in ancient times to the noble resistance of the people of Occupied Palestine in our own era, the enslaved and oppressed have sought to throw off the chains by which their masters keep them bound. The great libertarian theorist Murray Rothbard argued that the history of human civilizations is largely a struggle of liberty

1   Taki Theodoracopulous, The United States of Everywhere, *American Conservative,* March 10, 2003

2   Bool and Carlyle, *For Liberty*

3   Thomas Jefferson, *Notes on Virginia*

4   *Webster's Ninth New Collegiate Dictionary*, 1983.

against power with the latter gaining the upper hand with much greater frequency than the former. The great nineteenth century historian Lord John Acton insisted that power corrupts and absolute power corrupts absolutely. At no point has the truth of Acton's famous adage been demonstrated more strongly than in the last century. R. J. Rummel's monumental studies in a unique field that he chooses to label "democide," a term coined to describe the systematic slaughter of subjects by the states which rule over them, show that nearly one hundred seventy million persons were annihilated by "their" governments during the twentieth century alone. These figures exclude those killed in intra-state warfare. Reviewing the sorry record of the treatment of subjects by states, Rummel paraphrases Acton and concludes that "power kills, and absolute power kills absolutely".[5] In a similar vein, the Nobel Laureate economist Friedrich August von Hayek recognized that power comes most easily to the ruthless, treacherous, cunning and amoral. Those who achieve power are faced with constant challenges to their position of supremacy and are therefore driven to eliminate all those who can challenge their rule. The more concentrated power becomes, the more ruthless and deadly those who hold it will be. Hence, those who have held the greatest amount of power throughout history have also been history's "massest" of mass murderers-Stalin, Hitler, Mao and others of their ilk.

The greatest crimes are those committed by large disciplined organizations rather than solitary individuals. Arthur Koestler noted:

"...a series of fundamental misconceptions...which prevented (man) from learning the lessons of the past, and...now put his survival in question. The first of these..is putting the blame for man's predicament on his selfishness, greed, etc.; in a word, on the aggressive, self-assertive tendencies of the individual...I would like to

---

5   R. J. Rummell, *Power Kills* and *Death by Government*.

suggest that the integrative tendencies of the individual are incomparably more dangerous than his self-assertive tendencies."[6]

One need not reject the claims of a Hobbes or a Burke that humans are creatures of passion rather than reason to recognize that the most severe crimes perpetrated by individuals pale in comparison to those committed by organizations led by some sort of institutionalized authority. The modern serial killer is insignificant when contrasted with the death squad member or secret policeman. The greatest crimes of all are, of course, committed by the institution of the state, what Nietzsche characterized as a "cold monster". It is of the utmost importance to recognize that even persons of "normal" psychological make-up or moral temperament can be driven to act in the most atrocious ways when prodded by group norms or the direction of malignant leaders. This is borne out by the relevant studies in social psychology, particularly those of Stanley Milgram.[7] Hannah Arendt described this phenomena as "the banality of evil", a process whereby the most senseless and irrational forms of inhumanity acquire an aura of normalcy and take place within an atmosphere of dull mechanization.[8]

Various critiques of power, authority and the state have arisen throughout history. The European Enlightenment of the seventeenth and eighteenth centuries gave birth to the ideology of classical liberalism, which sought to limit the rule of power through various institutionalized mechanisms and processes. Classical anarchism arose as an ideology that explicitly rejected the authority of the state in toto rather than seeking to simply curb its worse abuses. In his study on the origins of the state, Franz Oppenheimer pointed out that states have their roots in

---

6   Arthur Koestler, *The Ghost in the Machine*

7   Stanley Milgram, *Obedience to Authority*

8   Hannah Arendt, *The Banality of Evil*

the invasion, conquest and plundering of some groups by others.[9] This observation strips the state of any veneer of legitimacy it may try to shroud itself with. Modern theorists of "democratic" or "constitutionalist" expressions of the state will typically argue that "modern" states are somehow to be differentiated from those of the Old Order, who claimed authority on the basis of divine right or superior might rather than "popular sovereignty", "the general will" or other such platitudes. Yet claims of this type have been effectively exposed and discredited by Lysander Spooner, Hans Hermann Hoppe and other notable anti-state thinkers.[10]

If the primary danger to human life and liberty is the excessive concentration of power, then humanity has never faced a greater threat than it does today as the universal dictatorship of the New World Order under the boot of American imperialism continues to be consolidated. At present, the American imperial regime demands the exclusive "right" of the first-use of military force, including nuclear weaponry, as part of its own "defensive" prerogative, yet curiously seeks to deny this right to others. In a manner rivaling the greatest tyrants in history, the US regime has systematically fabricated all sorts of extravagant falsehoods to justify its imperial ambitions regarding the Islamic nations. The American regime has established a Faustian bargain with the degenerate ideology of Zionism for the purpose of further consolidation of its own power, both internationally and within the American nation itself. The emerging world order is one of unilateral and utterly arbitrary rule by a regime that demands absolute obedience, economic domination by a handful of transnational corporations of the First World by means of mercantilist arrangements managed by byzantine bureaucracies, and cultural dominance by the combined values of liberal commercialism-consumerism and authoritarian leftist-egalitarianism and "multiculturalism" under the ideology of

9 Franz Oppenheimer, *The State*

10 Lysander Spooner, *No Treason* and Hans Hermann Hoppe, *Democracy: The God That Failed*

"political correctness." David Michael describes the dangers, both bellowing and subtle, posed by such a global order:

> "Even without the danger of the machinery of world government falling into the hands of a Stalin, Hitler or Pol Pot, and without the danger of large supranational institutions or nations being manipulated or exploited to serve certain groups or individuals at the expense of other groups or individuals, the sheer remoteness of supranational institutions from the ordinary people can have undesirable effects. The remoteness of decision making can lead to inappropriate decisions, as might occur where the quality of the food we eat is determined by supranational institutions rather than local farmers. The remoteness of the dominant culture can engender psychological and sociological problems-violence, alienation, crime and youth problems have been attributed, inter alia, to globalization and the breakdown of communities that it has engendered." [11]

As power has never been quite as centralized as it is at present, the anarchist critique is now more relevant than ever. The essence of the traditional anarchist position is that the state is no more than a criminal gang writ large. The state exists to control territory, protect an artificially privileged ruling class, exploit its subjects or expand its power. Any other claims by or on behalf of the state are simply a matter of evasion, obfuscation, or perhaps mere naiveté. Although the philosophical anarchist critique of the state originating from the ideas of William Godwin or Pierre Joseph Proudhon is the most radical and comprehensive, this critique follows in the footsteps of many strands of traditional ethical, religious and philosophical systems going back to very ancient times. These include the criticisms of power offered by the early Chinese philosopher Lao-tzu, the Stoic and Cynic branches of classical Greek philosophy, the very ancient Hebrew Scriptures, and the teachings of early Church fathers such as Augustine of

11   David E. Michael, A New Land, A New Life, A New Hope, *Voice of the Resistance*, Issue Two, February 2003.

Hippo as well as tendencies within the Radical Reformation, such as the Anabaptists.[12]

Having emerged only a couple of centuries ago and having never been dominant in any particular nation or culture, philosophical anarchism is still a rather new and underdeveloped political outlook. "Classical" anarchism of the nineteenth and early twentieth century variety, represented by Bakunin, Kropotkin and the Spanish anarcho-syndicalists, positioned itself as the most radical wing of the international socialist labor movement, as the so-called "labor question" was the dominant social struggle of the day. The political programs of the classical anarchists, as well as their contemporary "neo-anarchist" descendants, typically call for some sort of decentralized socialism, although neo-anarchism often focuses more on the advancement of left-wing cultural values such as feminism, "anti-racism" and "gay liberation" than on politico-economic matters. Another branch of modern anarchist thought, the "libertarian" anarchism of Murray Rothbard, is more rooted in classical liberalism than classical socialism, and traces its ancestry to the uniquely American branch of classical anarchism that emerged in the nineteenth century, the so-called "individualist" anarchism of Lysander Spooner and Benjamin R. Tucker. Although these variations of anarchist thought provide a rich intellectual heritage that can be drawn upon, they are clearly inadequate in a number of important ways. The principle error in the branches of anarchism thus far established is that of universalism. It is particularly important that this error be confronted if anarchism is to offer a viable alternative to the universalist ideology that provides the intellectual foundations of the New World Order.

Reading through the incessant manifestos and political statements issued by anarchist factions, one notices a number of dominant themes. Foremost among these are a type of Rousseauan

---

12   Colin Ward, *Anarchy in Action* and Harold Barlcay, *People without Government: The Anthropology of Anarchy*

utopianism that postulates the innate benevolence of human nature, a benevolence that would realize its potential if only the oppressive chains of established institutions were removed and the true essence of humanity allowed to flourish. As the nineteenth century was a time of enormous human advancement, classical anarchists like Proudhon or Bakunin can be forgiven for adopting such a childishly naive outlook. However, with the experience of the twentieth century now behind us, such a perspective becomes laughable with the advantage of hindsight. Another common theme in conventional anarchist thought is an implicit reliance on archaic Marxist and Fabian social democratic economic theory, a set of ideas that have been disastrous in every nation where they have been put into practice. Marxism is a dead faith, except among Western radicals, and the elitist social democratic views advanced by the Fabians have served to create a permanently entrenched "new class" of bureaucratic parasites that are slowly but surely driving the First World nations towards stagnation, deterioration and eventual collapse.[13] Anarchists are typically the most zealous champions of the cultural ideals of the modern Left-feminism, environmentalism, homosexualism, anti-racism. Yet these ideas are hardly radical in the modern welfare states of the West. Traditional forms of oppression such as bestial violence towards ethnic out-groups, the traditional religious subordination of women, and the organized state persecution of homosexuals have become socially unacceptable in modern societies to such a degree that Scotland Yard now maintains a "Diversity Directorate" to police attitudes not sanctioned by the high priests of "political correctness". Left-wing anarchists have, on such matters, become a type of self-parody that robotically parrots the rhetoric of the left-wing of the ruling class.

The professed aims of the anarchists of the Left are also in conflict with one another. The ideal political order postulated by left-anarchists is typically something that resembles a traditional New England town meeting or the participatory democracy of

---

13   Kevin A. Carson, The New Class' Will to Power: Liberalism and Social Control at http://www.attackthesystem.com

ancient Athens. While this model is no doubt as legitimate as any other, it is hardly any sort of panacea. After all, it was the democracy of Athens that put Socrates to death, thereby souring his successors Plato and Aristotle on democracy, and it was the town meeting governments of Puritan New England that instigated the witch trials of Salem. Yet, left-anarchists somehow assume that all of their idealized directly democratic, consensus-based, decentralized communities are somehow going to embrace the egalitarian-multicultural perspective of the Left. If such a system were put into place in Saudi Arabia tomorrow, the first vote taken would be to appoint Osama bin Laden to the position of President for Life. Libertarian anarchists make a similar mistake in their efforts to universalize a commercialist culture bound together by no common threads other than the actions of consumers in the marketplace and the standard common law rules concerning crimes, torts and contracts.

To understand what is wrong with these schools of anarchism, it may be useful to draw upon the work of Hayek. Loosely and awkwardly, we might characterize a Hayekian approach to social theory as one that draws a sharp distinction between "constructivist" and "organicist" understandings of social evolution and the origins of human institutions. Both leftist and libertarian variations of anarchist theory are implicitly rooted in Enlightenment rationalism, which tended to glorify and overstate the capacities of human reason and the ability of human beings to achieve a certain state of existence through the application of critical intelligence for the purpose of reconstructing the external world. While the excesses of the Enlightenment in this realm may have been an understandable backlash against the superstition and irrationalism that often dominated previous eras, the enduring legacy of all this has been a prevailing tendency towards fantastic utopianisms on the part of modern intellectuals, whether they be of the left-anarchist, left-liberal, libertarian, Marxist or neoconservative varieties. As an antidote, Hayek emphasized the inherent limitations of human knowledge and human reason as a means of "constructing" elaborate plans for the reorganization of society that are ultimately doomed to failure and the intellectual conceit reflected by such efforts.

One of the most distinguishing characteristics of anarchists is the smallness of their ranks. This is likely rooted in the tendency of most anarchists, of whatever school, to focus on ideological abstractions and a type of intellectual elitism that disregards the sentiments and sensibilities of ordinary people. Most people are not intellectuals. Most people are not interested in ideology. Most people are not the rugged self-reliant individualists idealized by libertarians or the faithful crusaders for social justice that serve as left-wing archetypes. Instead, the nature of most people is to focus on their immediate day-to-day business. Most people seek security, identity and self-actualization in groups and get their ideas about what constitutes "right and wrong" from cues taken from peers, members of their own in-groups and perceived leaders and authority figures. The strongest attachments of this type seem to be family, ethnicity, religion, culture, language, geography and, to some degree, economic function and social class. Particularistic attachments of these types are commonly disregarded by leftist and libertarian intellectuals (and by establishment liberals and neoconservatives!) as reactionary, backward, overly parochial or provincial, ignorant and superstitious and even bigoted and hateful. Yet it is precisely these types of particularism that provide the social glue that holds organic and authentic human societies and cultures together. It is these types of particularism that the ruling class of the New World Order wishes to eliminate in order to reduce every individual to the level of identity-less worker-consumer drone faithfully practicing the religion of the credit card and reciting the catechism of political correctness. Consequently, it is these particularisms and the attachments that ordinary people have to them that serve as humanity's best hope for fostering resistance to the universal slavery the oligarchs of the New World Order wish to bring about.

There remains the question as to how the anarchist critique is to be practically applied and what sort of institutions an anarchism-influenced civilization would likely produce. Unlike some of his successors, the godfather of classical anarchism Pierre Joseph Proudhon recognized that "anarchy" was an ideal, like "peace" or "justice", towards which humanity could only strive. Said Proudhon:

> "...It is scarcely likely, however far the human race may progress in civilization, morality and wisdom, that all traces of government and authority will vanish." [14]

Likewise, the eminent philosopher and mathematician Bertrand Russell characterized anarchism as "the ultimate ideal to which society should approximate".[15] Instead of pursuing utopian fantasies, anarchists should focus on identifying and breaking up concentrations of power wherever they may be located. The best bet for achieving this aim would likely be the development of strong regionalist and localist movements, both inside and outside of the territorial boundaries of the United States, with each of these reflecting the unique cultural or ideological orientations of their own organic or intentional communities, and organized in ways whereby different regions and communities are independent but mutually supportive of one another in the face of imperial power, regardless of their particular sectarian differences. The perspective of Troy Southgate offers a clue as to how to proceed:

> "We firmly believe in political, social and economic decentralization. In other words, we wish to see a positive downward trend whereby all bureaucratic concepts such as the UN, NATO, the EU and the World Bank and even nation-states like England and Germany are eradicated and consequently replaced by autonomous village communities." [16]

---

14   quoted in Barclay, *People without Government* p. 27.

15   quoted in Noam Chomsky, *Deterring Democracy* p. 398.

16   Troy Southgate, interviewed by Richard Hunt, from the Terra Firma web site at http://www.rosenoire.terrafirma.org

Such a vision is entirely compatible with the original anarchist vision of Proudhon who offered decentralized confederations of communities, municipalities and distinctive regions, each containing their own cultural identity, combined with an economy ordered on the basis of small property holders and dispersed control over resources, cooperatives and worker organizations. Such a vision affords most of humanity the opportunity to obtain sovereignty within the context of the social groups most strongly identified with. Such a vision offers a means of reconciling the numerous social conflicts fostered by the modern state resulting in an increase in social harmony, liberty, prosperity and peace. Those with conflicting values should simply separate from one another in favor of mutual self-segregation. Such is the way to authentic cultural diversity as opposed to the vision of those for whom "diversity" is simply a collection of exotic foods, museum displays and state-mandated social engineering.

As noted, anarchism as a political philosophy is still very much in the elementary stage of its development as an intellectual system. Fortunately, certain strands of anarchistic thought have emerged in recent years that may eventually prove to be a corrective for some of the extravagance and frivolity found in the established branches of anarchism. One of these is a tendency emerging from the British Far Right known as "National-Anarchism." This particular variation of anarchist theory lacks the irrational utopianism found in most other schools of anarchism. It might be said that national-anarchism is anarchy without pretensions. The core tenet of national-anarchist ideology is a fervent opposition to the emerging global system of the "New World Order" under the rule of American imperialism. More than any other political tendency, anarchist or otherwise, national-anarchism recognizes that there is really only one system of government in the contemporary world and that is the American empire. As a national-anarchist publication, "Voice of the Resistance," puts it:

"Nations, at least as you knew and loved them, are dead. We live today in a post-nationalist, globalized world. What you call your nation is now a mere administrative district of the New World Order. Never mind its 'proud and ancient history'! Never mind its 'wonderful accomplishments'! Never mind how many of your ancestors fought and died for it! Those things were in the past." [17]

Incidentally, this apt description of the nature of the New World Order applies to the American nation as well, despite the American origins of the global system. The conservative Catholic commentator Joseph Sobran observes:

"Only a few Americans have clearly understood that contrary to our sentimental illusions, the old federated constitutional republic has become not only a single consolidated state, but an empire as well. Today the president has ceased to be a mere executive, subordinate to the legislative branch, and has become an elective emperor, a temporary Caesar. This is hard for Americans to see, because it goes against our cherished national myths and has no close historical precedent. But foreigners may see it more clearly than we do. To American ears, the phrase "American imperialism" still sounds like leftist jargon. But it is more accurate than our slogans of democracy." [18]

American conservatives, libertarians and other anti-statists and anti-globalists now find themselves in an interesting ideological predicament. To consistently oppose "Big Government", one must first and foremost oppose centralized government, imperial government and global government. The foremost proponent of centralism, imperialism and globalism in today's world is the US regime. This necessitates that authentic anti-statists adopt an attitude that the jingoist wing of US politics would characterize as "anti-Americanism." As a look at the leading "paleoconservative" publications will show, this is a position that

---

17   *Voice of the Resistance*, Issue Two, February 2003.

18   Joseph Sobran, The Empire and Its Denizens, *The Wander*, May 15, 2003.

traditionalist conservatives are loathe to adopt. Their deathly fear of being labeled "anti-American" and lumped together with the riff raff of the reactionary left prevents them from developing as comprehensive a critique of the global imperial order as they otherwise might (just as their deathly fear of being labeled "anti-Semitic" prevents them from developing a similar critique of the role of Zionist ideology in the formulation of American imperial ambitions).[19] Yet these phobias are unfounded. If the historic America that traditionalist conservatives cling to is just another nation that has died at the hands of the empire, then the current US regime is not an expression of America but a hostile, enemy, occupational regime. Joseph Sobran notes:

"At any rate, the old America-the America of hard work and sound money, of thrift and piety, of small property and free markets, of individual freedom and responsibility, of limited government and dispersed power-is gone. The kind of people who made the old America hardly exists anymore. Their descendants might as well belong to another species; anyway, they will soon be outnumbered by aliens and "minorities"... Americans neither remember the old America nor comprehend the new one, which defies comprehension. What is an "American" these days? Someone who has filled out the proper forms? One out of hundreds of millions of disinherited people, who have nothing in common but a government that supplies them with depreciating paper currency? A mere digit of the empire, I suppose."[20]

---

19   For example, the colorful paleoconservative commentator Taki Theodoracopulous states: ...the recent antiwar demonstrations all over Europe were heartbreaking, at least for me. Basically the demonstrations were anti-American, no ifs or buts about it. I am very much against the war for the obvious reasons...The idea, however, that I'm on the same side with American-haters like the egregious Bianca Jagger makes my blood boil. Taki Theodoracopulous, The United States of Everywhere, American Conservative, March 10, 2003. The very same issue of American Conservative featured a particularly mediocre article by neoconservative ideologue John Derbyshire reviewing Kevin MacDonald's Culture of Critique, a work that exposes racist tendencies within Jewish culture. The piece was obviously included as Look, we're not anti-Semitic! window dressing. John Derbyshire, The Marx of the Anti-Semites, American Conservative, March 10, 2003.

20   Sobran, *The Empire*...

Serious opponents of global empire are not conservatives but radicals and revolutionaries of the first order. More than any other ideological tendency, national-anarchism recognizes that traditional ideological, cultural and even national boundaries are irrelevant in the current world order. As David Michael, a leading theoretician of national-anarchism, explains:

> "The 'left/right' political distinction is a cynical ploy to divide the people and set them against each other so that they do not unite against the single main enemy of us all: the Establishment. As Eduard Limonov remarked: 'There's no longer any left or right. There's the system and the enemies of the system.'" [21]

If traditional nations have been absorbed by the Empire, and if the traditional left/right political spectrum has been dissolved by the universalization of the values of American imperialism and global capital, then the traditionalist elements of the right are the natural allies of the anti-corporate left. The primary divisions among these scattered forces are cultural in origin. The traditional right places its emphasis on established institutions and values such as family, religion, ethnicity, nationality, traditional culture and organic communities. The left focuses first and foremost on those social groups believed to have been previously dispossessed or "excluded" in some way. These include workers and the poor, racial minorities, women, homosexuals and others. This type of progressivism has become institutionalized and rigidified in its own right as the existence of Scotland Yard's Diversity Directorate and the "speech codes" found on the campuses of American universities demonstrate. Both sides on these matters regard their opponents as tyrants and reactionaries. If effective opposition to the New World Order necessarily involves the creation of an anti-Establishment alliance that transcends conventional ideological, cultural and national boundaries, then obviously some means of accommodating such a diverse array of

---

21   David E. Michael, Unity in Diversity, *Voice of the Resistance*, Issue One, October 2002.

182

perspectives is sorely needed. National-anarchism invokes the ideal of radical decentralization as a means to this end. As "Voice of the Resistance" states:

"Consider the ancient Greek polis or city-state. Here was an institution that truly allowed for diversity of government. Although no overarching state structure existed, a variety of communities thrived across ancient Greece, often with very different systems of government ranging from the quasi-democracies of Athens to the more communistic regimes of Sparta. It is not too difficult to envisage an adapted form of such a system as an alternative to the American imperialism of the modern age. This, surely, must be anarchism at its most practicable and useful."

"Let a thousand different communities flourish! Let those who want communism have communism! Let those who want Islam have Islam! Let those who want Christianity have Christianity! Let those who want to live among their own racial kind do so! Let even those who want to keep the sham democracies of American imperialism have them! But let us all unite to defend such diversity, such freedom, against the tyranny of the bland capitalism espoused by our lords and masters and their media puppets."[22]

National-anarchism of the type described here is a marked improvement over prior expressions and applications of anarchist theory. National-anarchism lacks the utopian fantasies employed by traditional left-wing anarchism and instead employs a heavy dose of realism. The contradictory nature of the conventional left-anarchist demand for decentralization, communal socialism and proletarian supremacy combined with the universalization of left-wing cultural values is absent from national-anarchism. Political decentralization would result in more rather than less social discrimination as there would be

---

22   *Voice of the Resistance*, Issue One, October 2002.

no centralized state to enforce egalitarian or progressive values within local communities. Likewise, the poor and working class tend to be the most socially conservative cultural element. Secularism, feminism, multiculturalism and homosexualism are the predominant social values of the cultural elite rather than the common people. Economic collectivism requires maximum social discipline and conformity. There is a reason why highly collectivist regimes, such as those of the Marxist-Leninist variety, severely repress political dissidents, religious believers and perceived sexual deviates.

Much of what passes for left-wing anarchism would, if implemented, is anything but anarchistic. Consider, for example, the political outlook of an outfit called the Northeastern Federation of Anarcho-Communists (NEFAC):

> "As anarcho-communists, we struggle for a classless, stateless, and non-hierarchical society. We envision an international confederation of directly democratic, self-managed communities and workplaces; a society where all markets, exchange value, systems of wages and divisions of labor have been abolished and the means of production and distribution are socialized in order to allow for the satisfaction of human needs, adhering to the communist principle: 'From each according to ability, to each according to need'." [23]

What we have here is simply a restatement of traditional Marxism with some nominally anarchistic ideas thrown in for good measure. How is this "international federation" going to be somehow different from a state? What if some communities in this federation decide to withdraw? Is an anarcho-Abe Lincoln going to come along to prevent them from doing so? What if some "directly democratic, self-managed communities and workplaces" do not want to abolish "all markets, exchange

---

23   *The Northeastern Anarchist*, Issue Four, Spring/Summer 2002.

value, systems of wages and division of labor"? How are "the means of production" going to be "socialized in order to allow for the satisfaction of human needs" without either a consumer market or a state plan? What about those people who do not wish to contribute "according to ability" but prefer to take more than their "need"? Who is going to say otherwise? It becomes clear that for NEFAC "anarchism" is simply a world communist government with a centrally planned economy of the type that has typically failed miserably in Marxist states. This becomes clear in an overview found in the NEFAC publication of the economic arrangements established by the anarcho-syndicalists of 1930s Spain:

> "Had the Spanish collectives been moving in a genuinely communist direction the tendency towards self-sufficiency and autonomy for each collective... would have been reversed in favor of centralized planning by delegate bodies." [24]

It is the precisely the decentralist and most anarchistic aspects of the Spanish anarcho-syndicalist collectives that are being condemned. Of course, the NEFAC group represents the intellectual bottom of the barrel even among the reactionary left. The ideas of all socialist-anarchists are not always so muddled and incoherent. The "libertarian" or "anarcho-capitalist" variations of anarchist theory are usually better well-developed than those of their left-wing counterparts. Economic problems and matters of practical application aside, a principal difficulty with "free market" anarchism is its reliance on abstract ideological concepts and indifference to cultural matters. Libertarians of this type make the same mistake as the Marxists who view everything from the perspective of a narrow economic determinism and intellectual constructs. The primary strength of national-anarchism is its rejection of universalism in favor of particularism. Adherents of national-anarchism are not required to accept any particular set of philosophical or cultural values

---

24   Anarchist Economics, Subversion, *The Northeastern Anarchist*, Issue Four, Spring/ Summer 2002.

beyond the bare minimum of opposition to the New World Order and the need to replace it with decentralized, community based political institutions. David Michael comments:

"One of the really neat things about national-anarchism is that it can appeal to a lot of very different people. Whether you're a communist, a nationalist, a Muslim, a Christian, or whatever, if you go along with the basic core ideas, such as opposition to the American-led 'New World Order', opposition to global governance by a one-world super state (de jure or de facto), and a belief in a world of small, relatively independent communities, each 'doing its own thing', then national-anarchism could appeal to you.... national-anarchism, by its very nature, allows its adherents to hold to a wide variety of peripheral values (Islamic, communist, Christian, Satanist and so forth)." [25]

Theoretically, then, national-anarchism could include not only the kinds of communities mentioned above but also communities organized according to the variations of classical anarchism (mutualism, syndicalism or anarcho-communism), neo-anarchism (primitivism, libertarian municipalism or the ideas of Lorenzo Komboa Ervin), libertarianism (whether of the Rothbardian, Randian or Hayekian variety), racial nationalism (including such tendencies within all races), various populist tendencies (such as the US militia movement or the Swedish National Democrats), monarchism (such as that favored by certain elements among the indigenous peoples of Hawaii) or the traditional tribe and clan based cultures found in African, Asian or Middle Eastern societies. Even ideological groupings that theoretically endorse a powerful centralized state (such as Marxist-Leninists or National Socialists) could achieve sovereignty within their own enclaves. Those who wish to retain some variation of the present system could do so. Those who favor a radically different system could, to a large degree, realize their

---

25   David E. Michael, National-Anarchist FAQ, from the nationalanarchist.com web site.

goals as well. National-anarchism focuses on cultural struggles, community sovereignty and authentic cultural diversity rather than economic determinism, abstract intellectual constructs or utopian egalitarianism and universalism.

Probably the most controversial aspect of national-anarchism is the fact that many of its leading theoreticians and adherents have their political roots in the British Far Right and have been previously involved with anti-immigration and white nationalist tendencies like the National Front or the International Third Position. Some national-anarchists continue to hold what might be characterized as, for lack of a better term, "conservative" views on race and culture. As Troy Southgate, the founder of national-anarchism, explains:

> "Racial miscegenation, for example, is viewed by National-Anarchists, as something which runs contrary to nature. Similarly, we regard issues like human cloning, euthanasia, homosexuality, genetically-modified foodstuffs, vivisection and abortion in the same way...(O)ur vision is based upon the realities of self-determination for all peoples and not on mindless racial hatred toward others. Furthermore, we do not subscribe to a supremacist agenda or wish to enforce our world view on others...These are issues which must be decided by those concerned, although we do remain adamant that such practices remain outside of our own naturally-based Anarchic communities...if people disagree...(w)e have no problem with that. As long as they do not prevent us from occupying our own space and land in which to live according to our own principles and beliefs. Those who attempt to interfere with our way of life or prevent us from realizing our distinct vision based upon Natural Order are nothing short of fascistic and authoritarian. We do not wish to persecute others or bend them to our will. Let them found their own communities..." [26]

---

26   Troy Southgate, interviewed by Hunt.

This outlook is a refreshing alternative to the anti-intellectualism and pseudo-Marxist totalitarianism offered by left-wing anarchists and the aristocratic, robber baron conservatism offered by anarcho-capitalists. With national-anarchist arrangements, controversial social questions could be resolved by means of community preference. There could be communities for separatists within all the different ethnic and religious groups along with multi-ethnic and secular communities. There could be pro-abortion and anti-abortion communities, gay militant and "homophobe" communities, gun nut and anti-gunner communities, vegan and carnivore communities, druggie and anti-druggie communities. Theoretically, there could be communities for UFO worshippers or human sacrifice enthusiasts. Some communities could be as closed as those of the Taliban or the Nazis while others could be as free-wheeling as the Mardi gras. Those who did not like the communities they found themselves in could simply migrate to a more appealing community.

Such a vision, what David Michael describes as an anarchy of "nations" or "homelands" or "communities", seems to be a realistic alternative to those forms of anarchism that promise the fulfillment of utopian fantasies of absolute social equality and social harmony or absolute individual sovereignty where every person somehow functions as a sovereign nation unto themselves. Such a vision seems entirely compatible with any consistent application of the traditional anarchist ideals of decentralization, anti-statism, mutual aid, voluntarism, individual sovereignty, free association and federation and community self-determination. However, because of the views of some leading theoreticians and adherents of national-anarchism on racial and cultural matters, the typical reaction of left-wing anarchists to national-anarchism has been rather similar to what one might expect from a five-year-old girl who suddenly discovers a gargantuan spider in her bed. But such hysteria is more illustrative of typical left-wing bigotry and narrow-mindedness rather than any actual weakness in the national-anarchist perspective.

For the record, I am not nor have I ever been either a racial separatist or a social conservative. On a purely personal level, an individual's race, religion or sexual orientation is no more important to me than their hair or eye color. Politically, my approach is fairly eclectic. Race is no doubt a factor in the determination of individual character and social relations, but so too is class, gender, religion, individual psychological traits, geography, culture, history, educational methods, parenting methods, life experience, probably physics and many other things. I would not prioritize race in the same manner as the above statements by Troy Southgate indicate. However, Southgate's views on Natural Order are relatively similar to those found among many nationalist or separatist tendencies among non-whites, most traditional religions, traditional indigenous cultures that leftists tend to romanticize, and much of the Old Left (which often regarded feminism as bourgeoisie and homosexuality as a manifestation of capitalist decadence). Many social groups that leftists claim to champion-urban American black males, rank and file union members, the oppressed masses of the Islamic world-would include within their ranks many people with such an outlook. All ethnic groups have their separatist, preservationist tendencies along with their assimilationist, integrationist tendencies just as all religions have their fundamentalist or traditionalist as well as their ecumenical tendencies. If it is acceptable for left-wing environmentalists to seek to preserve the tiniest micro-species, then why is it not acceptable for some people to wish to preserve traditional races, nationalities, religions, languages or cultures? If the destruction of the Baghdad Museum and Library is rightfully viewed as a crime against culture, then why is the extinction of unique ethnic identities to be casually dismissed? While an interest in the preservation of specific ethnic groups does not have to mean that new ones cannot evolve, would the world really be a better place if everyone were beige?

On social matters, I tend to follow the lead of the late Ernest Van den Haag, who for many years was a leading American conservative intellectual and part of the circle of staunch Cold War militarists associated with William F. Buckley Jr. and the National Review magazine. Van den Haag was a harsh critic of leftists and libertarians alike and held right-wing social democratic views not unlike those of today's neoconservatives. He was also a fervent proponent of "law and order" and vigorously defended the death penalty and the strict punishment of criminals. Yet, Van den Haag also supported the "right-to-die," abortion rights, decriminalization of drugs and prostitution and eventually reversed his earlier position of support for the censorship of pornography. He also remarked that society has no compelling interest in regulating or legislating concerning the matter of homosexuality. While I am an anti-imperialist and an anarcho-socialist rather than a conservative like Van den Haag, I largely share his social outlook. He was no doubt drawing on the experience of his own native Holland, a nation that maintains what are likely the most "liberal" policies in these matters and a nation that I have visited myself and found to be rather harmonious, prosperous and attractive.

It seems to me that efforts to eliminate abortion are simply futile. Many American social and religious conservatives lament the famed 1973 "Roe v. Wade" Supreme Court decision that legalized abortion in the early stages of pregnancy and rail incessantly about the number of abortions that have occurred since then, yet abortion remains illegal in Mexico but that nation has a higher rate of abortions per capita annually than the US. Reinstituting the legal ban on abortions would likely be about as effective as the legal ban on psychoactive drugs. The ancient Greeks seem to have had literally no conception of sexual morality and homosexuality was apparently the virtual norm in ancient Greece, at least among the elites, yet classical Greek culture is regarded by many as the apex of Western civilization, particularly and ironically by many conservatives. On euthanasia, I draw a sharp distinction between voluntary euthanasia and involuntary euthanasia. On one hand, if a terminally ill or severely physically disabled person wishes to end their own life and others wish to assist them, I can see no objection to that. Yet, I do not consider it to ever be appropriate for someone to take it upon themselves to kill another person without their consent and call it "mercy killing" or whatever, though I certainly think that such acts should not be penalized nearly as severely as homicides committed during the course of common crimes. On ecological questions, I take a somewhat more moderate position than that of many radicals. I largely agree with the conclusions of former Greenpeace activist Bjorn Lomborg,[27] who regards the fears of modern environmentalists as greatly exaggerated. I am considerably less sanguine about human cloning and genetic engineering, conjuring as they do the images of the eugenicist ideals of Hitler, Pol Pot and Imperial Japan.

Of course, all of the aforementioned questions are of an endlessly controversial nature with fervent and emotional opinions being held on all sides. Anarchistic political institutions provide a means for such disputes to be settled as peacefully as possible. Those with conflicting values or ideals should simply go their own way. Webster's Dictionary defines anarchism as "a political theory holding all forms of governmental authority to be unnecessary and undesirable and advocating a society based on voluntary cooperation and free association of individuals and groups." The catch is that people with different values or goals will form different kinds of associations. Egalitarians will form egalitarian associations. Elitists will form elitist associations. Socialists will form socialist associations. Racialists will form racialist associations. It may be that such absolute voluntarism can be maintained only as an ideal to be striven for. Obviously, the next best thing is radically decentralized politics. Such decentralization would likely result in the vast ideological and cultural diversity favored by national-anarchists. It is not all that difficult to envision how a system of political, cultural and geographical decentralization might work. However, for this kind of decentralization to exist as a concrete reality rather than as a

---

27   Bjorn Lomborg, *The Skeptical Environmentalist*

theoretical construct only, economic decentralization would have to take place as well. Otherwise, political/cultural/geographical decentralization would exist only on paper. Consider, for example, the US constitutional system. Formally, the government of the United States is organized on the basis of a separation of powers, both vertically and horizontally. The national government consists of three separate and distinct branches-the legislative, executive and judicial-with executive power spread out through a myriad of bureaucracies. The national government ostensibly shares power with the semi-autonomous state governments who maintain a similar separation of powers and delegate certain authority to localities. The enforcement arm of government is divided into the courts, the prosecutor's office, the police, the lawyer's guilds, and the penal system, with each of these being theoretically independent of one another. The military functions as a semi-autonomous state with its own legal system and governmental structure (much like the medieval church), but is still subject to external civilian authority. As sophisticated as this entire state apparatus may be, all of it is still controlled at the top by those with economic power in the broader society (Big Business, Big Banking, Big Oil, armaments manufacturers and other corporate interests) and a variety of well-organized and financially well-endowed interest groups (bureaucrats' unions, professional associations, Zionists and other ethnic/religious interests and single-issue pressure groups like "pro-life" and "pro-choice). As Jaroslaw Tomasiewicz states:

> "A pluralistic, decentralized society can be the only alternative to a unified and centralized New World Order, a formless plasma fed on pop culture. Not only does territorial decentralization (broadening the authority of communities and regions) have to occur but also different cultural communities should gain autonomy. Not only the state but also every community should have the opportunity to proclaim its own laws for its own people. In that situation, coexistence of traditional patriarchal families and feminists' or homosexual pairs, religious

fundamentalists' communities and countercultural groups, military-racist communities of the right wing and anarchistic or communistic groups of the left wing would be possible. So that the territorial and cultural decentralization doesn't become a fiction, it has to be accompanied by economic decentralization and that would mean eliminating the concentration of property and production forms. The information technology revolution gives the opportunity to make this process real. I believe that this idea of a pluralistic society is the only program, which would be able to combine so many scattered and quarrelling sections of anti-System opposition. The only requirement for accepting it is surrendering the ambition of making the whole of humanity happy by your own idea (It will be enough if you concentrate on making yourself happy only)." [28]

This vision outlined by Tomasiewicz intersects nicely with the original anarchist ideal offered by Pierre Joseph Proudhon, a man whose ideas illustrate that one can be both an extreme radical and an extreme conservative simultaneously. For this kind of Left-Right convergence to emerge in the modern world, a mutual cease-fire and non-aggression pact would have to be established among competing cultural groups with political decentralization and mutual self-segregation utilized as a means of dealing with irresolvable disputes. Economic decentralization is somewhat more problematical given the technical questions involved. While in decentralist, pluralist social systems different types of communities would have widely divergent economic arrangements contingent upon their own needs, traditions and ideological orientations, it would seem that certain common economic principles could and should be agreed upon by the various anti-System forces. The principle conflicts involve the role of the state in economic matters and the historic dispute between the laissez faire and socialist traditions. The ranks of

28   Jaroslaw Tomasciewicz, An Alternative to the American Empire of the New World Order at http://www.attackthesystem.com/alternative.html

economic radicals include anarcho-syndicalists, mutualists, guild socialists, councilists, agrarians, primitivists, distributists, anarcho-communists, and adherents of social credit, geoists, populists and others. The common thread among all of these tendencies is a belief that economic power and control over resources, property and productive processes should be dispersed and devoid of centralism. Economic decentralization is a natural complement to political decentralization and vice versa. [29]

When considering these ideas, it is interesting to consider their relevance to authentically American cultural history and traditions. It is a great irony, and perhaps an illustration of a fatal contradiction in the American psyche, that a nation originally founded by explorers, pioneers, mercenaries, pirates and refugees, established by means of an anti-colonial revolution, the principle exponent of the intellectual culture of the Enlightenment, structured on a decentralist, federalist basis, should degenerate after only two centuries into an imperialist empire ordered on crass commercialism and consumerism, intellectual mediocrity, conformity and murderous neo-colonial aggression. The decentralist, anti-imperialist sympathies and immense respect for an authentic plurality of cultures found in national-anarchist thought are perfectly in keeping with early American traditions and classical American ideals. The isolation of North America allowed those who wished to escape persecution in Europe to find a homeland in the New World. Puritans went to Massachusetts, Baptists to Rhode Island, and Quakers to Pennsylvania. Virginia and the Carolinas were largely colonies established by merchants and sea traders. Georgia was a penal colony a la Botany Bay. The American Revolution of 1776 came from a desire on the part of the colonists to preserve the freedom and independence they had found in America from the creeping tyranny of the Crown. [30] The westward expansion involved the creation of settlements organized

---

29 Kevin A. Carson, The Iron Fist behind the Invisible Hand at http://www.mutualist.net. Keith Preston, What Would an Anarcho-Socialist Economy Look Like? at http://www. attackthesystem.com/economy.html

30 Murray N. Rothbard, *Conceived in Liberty*

as anarchistically as any ever found.[31] Along the way there has been the Southern independence movement of the Confederacy, slave revolts, labor uprisings, and massive resistance to imperialist wars and conscription. It is this aspect of American history and culture that modern revolutionaries should appeal to and capitalize on. Judging by the standards of classical American ideals, the modern US regime is nothing more than one massive act of treason.

It is also interesting to note the compatibility of national-anarchist ideals with those of authentic resistance movements that have emerged from the grassroots of American society in recent years. Many in the militia/patriot/constitutionalist milieu have worked to form their own intentional communities governed by the ideological principles of their choice. Others have created an alternative governmental or legal infrastructure based on the US Constitution, the Confederate Constitution, state constitutions, the Bible, the Magna Carta, old English common law, the Articles of Confederation, the Northwest Ordinance and other sources of perceived cultural authority.[32] Some, like the Christian Jural Societies or the Continental Congress, have created a separatist or provisional political structure in the same way that the Palestinians established their own national organizational structure, Parliament and all, in the face of exile and the expropriation of their homeland by Zionist invaders. The national-anarchist concept of small, seceded communities emerging in the face of the global super state is also consistent with the ideas postulated by some of the more radical libertarian thinkers, particularly Murray Rothbard and the leading contemporary exponent of Rothbardian anarchism, Hans Hermann Hoppe. Like the national-anarchists, Hoppe is a harsh critic of modern systems of liberal democracy. Like the national-anarchists, Hoppe regards the universalization of American imperialism and liberal democracy to be the primary threat to freedom and liberty. His book, "Democracy: The

---

31 Terry Anderson and P. J. Hill, An Experiment in Anarcho-Capitalism: The Not So Wild West, 3 *Journal of Libertarian Studies* 9, 1979.

32 Joel Dyer, *Harvest of Rage*

God That Failed" is a landmark work in political philosophy and political economy. [33] Hoppe regards modern democracy as degeneration from earlier monarchical systems which he regards as less wasteful and warlike. When the stable, prosperous monarchy of Liechtenstein is compared with the indebted, near bankrupt, rapidly deteriorating social democratic states that dominate Europe, we can see that Hoppe may be on to something. [34] Some national-anarchist sympathizers express monarchist tendencies as well. Rothbard believed the right of political secession to be among the most powerful bulwarks against state tyranny. As a staunch anti-militarist and anti-imperialist, Rothbard believed that only two wars in American history were "just" wars-the American Revolution and the Southern War of Independence of 1861-1865. This position is consistent with that of the early American anarchist Lysander Spooner, an anti-slavery lawyer who championed southern secession while at the same time calling for slave insurrections against the southern aristocracy.

If only the South had won the US Civil War, there would have been no consolidated national regime, and therefore no American entry into World War I, no Treaty of Versailles, no Hitler, no World War II, no Holocaust, no Stalinist occupation of Eastern Europe, no Cold War, no arms race, no Korean War and no War in Vietnam. Indeed, it would appear that the failure of the Confederate States of America was one of the greatest tragedies in world history. Applying these principles of secession and sovereignty to the modern world, it becomes obvious that anti-imperialists must stand by all nations and movements who defy the New World Order. This means defending Iraq, Palestine, Afghanistan, Venezuela, Cuba, Libya, Yemen, Syria, Somalia, the Sudan, Iran, North Korea, Lebanon and any other nations who display resistance, regardless of what one may think of their internal politics. It means standing by nations like Russia, Germany, France, Turkey and Belgium when they refuse

---

33   Keith Preston, Democracy as Tyranny at http://www.attackthesystem.com/hoppe.html

34   Karen De Coster, Will Liechtenstein Autonomy Prevail?, Mises Institute, April 28, 2003. http://www.mises.org/fullstory.asp?control=1214

the dictates of American imperialism, even if this is largely an intramural dispute within the ranks of the masters of the New World Order. It means supporting armed insurrectionary movements on the periphery, such as the FARC of Colombia, the Peoples' War Group of Nepal, the Shining Path of Peru, the Zapatistas of Chiapas, Hamas, Hezbollah, the ETA, IRA and the Corsican autonomists.

Hoppe's views on secession also involve a preference for small communities. Critiquing the failure of the Confederacy, Hoppe argues that the Union refused to allow the secession because the loss of revenue, subjects and territory involved was simply more costly to itself than fighting a war "to preserve the Union". As an alternative, a modern secessionist effort should:

"...take its cues from the European Middle Ages when, from about the twelfth century until well into the seventeenth century (with the emergence of the modern central state), Europe was characterized by the existence of hundreds of free and independent cities, interspersed into a predominately feudal social structure. By choosing this model and striving to create a U.S. punctuated by a large and increasing number of territorially disconnected free cities-a multitude of Hong Kongs, Singapores, Monacos and Liechtensteins strewn out over the entire continent-two otherwise unattainable but central objectives can be accomplished. First, besides recognizing the fact that the liberal-libertarian potential is distributed highly unevenly across the country, such a strategy of piecemeal withdrawal renders secession less threatening politically, socially and economically. Second, by pursuing this strategy simultaneously at a great number of locations all over the country, it becomes exceedingly difficult for the central state to create a unified opposition in public opinion to the secessionists which would secure the level of popular support and voluntary cooperation necessary for a successful crackdown." [35]

---

[35]   Hans Hermann Hoppe, *Democracy: The God That Failed.*

Of course, it is important to realize that Hoppe is proceeding from a totally different set of ideological presumptions than those of the national-anarchists. Hoppe is clearly in the liberal-Enlightenment tradition while national-anarchists are critical of modernity in a way that is similar to that of traditional conservatives in the Burkean tradition, notably Russell Kirk. Also, Hoppe is primarily interested in a more uniform liberal-libertarian-capitalist ideological secession while national-anarchists favor a proliferation of communities that span the ideological and cultural spectrum. The national-anarchist position appears to be the preferable one, as it is more conducive to the kind of diversity that would be necessary to make such efforts viable. Hoppe's views on secession are very similar to those of David Michael. Unlike many leftist or libertarian anarchists, Michael does not reject electoral action, demonstrations, infiltration or "lone wolf" actions out of hand. Michael is refreshingly pragmatic and methodical when it comes to questions of strategy.[36] While favoring a "fight on all fronts" approach, Michael's primary emphasis is on acquiring territory, resources and influence and building communities and alliances. On the question of alliances, Michael comments:

> "Many groups are opposed to globalization-often for different reasons: anarchists, national-anarchists, nationalists, Islamic fundamentalists, Maoists, national Bolsheviks, national socialists, national revolutionaries, third positionists, environmentalists...As globalization and American imperialism tighten their grip upon the world we might wonder whether the old, and largely redundant, distinction between 'left' and 'right' in politics might be replaced by a new and far more bitter struggle: the struggle between the global Establishment-the monopolar New World Order, dominated by America and American neoliberal economics and values-and those many and varied people who oppose it."[37]

---

36   Michael, *A New Land…*

37   Michael, continued.

In the process of building communities and homelands, David Michael suggests a number of core conditions that need to be met. Such projects must be adequate in size, involve enough people and involve people of high quality and commitment. Geographical isolation is also a necessity, along with ideological isolation, the avoidance of provocation of external authorities, an absence of destructive ideological or personality traits among the participants and a resolute commitment to the avoidance of efforts to dominate other communities. Michael notes:

> "Certain of our fellow travelers in the struggle against the Establishment have imperialist potential. The communists, National Socialists, and Islamic fundamentalists-all of these are fighting against the New World Order. Yet each, if it were to triumph all over the earth, has the potential to produce a globalised world order every bit as sinister as that of the current American empire. Care needs to be taken, when working with such people, that in working with them for the destruction of the Establishment, we do not inadvertently work towards the replacement of one globalizing or imperialist force with another." [38]

We might also remember that is has been precisely these types of internecine battles among rival revolutionary factions that have destroyed prior revolutionary efforts, such as those of France of 1789, Russia of 1917, Spain of 1936 and Paris of 1968. David Michael's warnings concerning these matters echo those of Bakunin, whose foresight regarding the inherent statist and centralist tendencies of the Marxists offered a prophetic vision of the horrors and tragedies that were to emerge in the twentieth century. As a means of avoiding the replacement of one kind of imperialism with another, we might once again return to the lessons of classical anarchism and learn from the example of the First International. The Marxists favored the concentration of power into the hands of the International's General Council,

---

38   Michael, continued.

which they had control over, while the Bakuninists (who comprised a majority of the International's membership) believed the International should be a model for the future post-revolutionary society with as much autonomy as possible afforded to the local sections. Similarly, the alliance against the New World Order should be radically decentralized. Just as the International maintained sections in various countries, each with their own specific ideological inclinations, so should an alliance against Anglo-Zionist imperialism be structured in such a way as to reflect the varying ideological and cultural currents found within distinctive communities, regions and nations.

I am not particularly knowledgeable of the cultural map of Europe or Asia beyond the purely elementary level. However, I might be able to provide a sketch of how such an alliance might be formed in North America, "in the belly of the beast," as Guevara said. America, Canada and Mexico each include a number of distinctive regions. In the US, the primary regions are the Northeast corridor, long time home of the mercantile trade and banking interests, the Southern "Bible Belt", a hot bed of religious fundamentalism and social conservatism, the Midwest, with its inclinations towards heartland populism, the West, still a bastion of Marlboro country individualism, and the Left Coast, a multicultural region with many diverse ethnic and religious populations and a reputation as a haven for "alternative" lifestyles.

Breaking things down a bit further, the rural and small town communities within America tend to lean towards social and cultural conservatism while the urban, metropolitan areas are more inclined towards "liberalism" and "progressivism". It is instructive to note the ideological content of various secessionist and decentralist movements that have appeared in the US in recent years. A San Francisco newspaper published an editorial calling for secession by that city and the creation of a liberal-progressive city-state, citing Iceland as a model. A still small but growing neo-secessionist movement in the old Confederate states claims Christianity and conservative Southern heritage as its banners. A libertarian-capitalist group, the Free State Project, wishes to colonize an American state and set about the business of eliminating its government. During the 1970s some in the hippie movement undertook an effort to colonize Vermont with some apparent success, as anyone familiar with the internal politics of Vermont is no doubt aware. The white separatist tendencies in the US have at times subscribed to a doctrine called "Northwest Imperative", the aim of which would be to establish a white nationalist homeland in the Northwestern United States. Similarly, the Black Nationalist Nation of Islam organization has long called for a sovereign black homeland within the borders of the US. While Europe is more traditionally homogenous and less pluralistic than America, no doubt similar arrangements can be found in European society as well. Troy Southgate notes that a number of the tendencies in the national-anarchist family tree, such as the National Front and the English Nationalist Movement, called for regional independence for the distinctive regions among the British Isles and, despite a strong anti-immigration stance, cooperation with black and Asian communities within Britain.[39] Independence movements exist in northern Italy, Flanders, Corsica, the Basque country and, of course, Northern Ireland.

All of this brings us back to the original vision of Thomas Jefferson. At the risk of grotesque oversimplification, we might characterize American political history as an ongoing battle between the decentralist, agrarian ideals of Jefferson and the mercantilist, centralist preferences of his rival, Alexander Hamilton. Indeed, we might regard the establishment of the US national state in its earliest, late eighteenth century form as the first triumph of the Hamiltonians over the Jeffersonians, an event where the far more libertarian and decentralized Articles of Confederation was replaced via mercantilist coup with the more centralist, presidential form of government with which

39   Southgate, *Transcending the Beyond: From Third Positionism to National-Anarchism*

Americans are familiar. Subsequent American history has dramatically illustrated the wisdom of the early anti-federalist critics of the US Constitution, such as Jefferson and Patrick Henry. The Jeffersonians went on to suffer severe military defeat during the US Civil War of 1861-65 and Hamiltonian mercantilism and state capitalism continued to tighten its grip on America. Mark Winchell observes:

> "By 1930, the Hamiltonian vision had triumphed everywhere in the United States except for the South and a few isolated pockets of rural culture elsewhere in the country...The Agrarians, however, believed that the Faustian bargain being offered to the south would result in the region giving up too much for too little. (It is doubtful that even they could have imagined the contemporary Sunbelt, with indistinguishable shopping malls stretching from Phoenix to Atlanta and a landscape of high-rise hotels with revolving restaurants on top.)" [40]

The early Jeffersonian vision of a republic of republics, with governmental systems ordered on the basis of counties divided into wards, and political leadership drawn from the ranks of natural aristocrats who achieved their position through superior ability, intelligence and character, with distinct communities achieving self-determination, includes a core set of ideas whose evolution continues through the work of Proudhon and Kropotkin, godfathers of British Distributism like G. K. Chesterton and Hilaire Belloc, traditionalist American conservatives such as Richard Weaver and M. E. Bradford, libertarians like Karl Hess and, today, the national-anarchist movement. To be a Jeffersonian in the America of today is to be both an extreme radical and, in a sense, an extreme reactionary. A modern Jeffersonian, in any authentic sense, is a "conservative revolutionary" of the first order. Norman Mailer, a self-described "Left-Conservative", characterizes such an outlook as "thinking in the style of Karl

---

40   Mark Royden Winchell, This Land Is Your Land, *American Conservative*, July 14, 2003.

Marx in order to attain certain values suggested by Edmund Burke." Mark Winchell continues:

> "Certainly, one of the challenges now facing any political philosophy is to find a way to achieve harmony in an increasingly pluralistic society. Properly understood, the qualities of diversity and tolerance are more natural to a conservative than a schematic leftist mindset. Among his 'six canons of conservative thought,' (Russell) Kirk identifies an 'affection for the proliferating variety and mystery of traditional life as distinguished from the narrowing uniformity and equalitarianism and utilitarian aims of most radical systems.' Decentralization-political, cultural, and economic-is one way of maintaining and enhancing that proliferating variety." [41]

Samuel Francis has speculated that paleoconservatives may be mistaken in adopting the label of "conservative". What is it about the world order of modern times that anyone should wish to conserve? The ideals of the paleocons and the national-anarchists converge on a number of key points-regionalism, localism, agrarianism, traditionalism. The vociferous anti-Americanism of the national-anarchists may trigger an instinctively negative reflex among those paleocons who regard themselves as patriots, but is the America which the national-anarchists reject so fervently the America of either classical Jeffersonian or contemporary paleoconservative ideals? Obviously not. Perhaps Francis is right. [42] Perhaps those modern thinkers who find inspiration in classical American values are not conservatives at all, but anarchists. Benjamin R. Tucker once remarked that if Jefferson had been alive in his own era (this was the late nineteenth century!), he would have been an anarchist. Indeed, the iconic conservative sociologist Robert Nisbet expressed admiration for the communitarian ideals championed by classical anarchists like

---

41   Winchell, continued.

42   It should be pointed out that Francis is a social nationalist and not an anarchist.

Kropotkin. And for those who wish to preserve both authentic diversity and distinctive communities, both inside and outside the territorial United States, national-anarchism does indeed offer a way. Indeed, it might not be too much of a stretch to say that national-anarchism is paleoconservatism taken to its logical conclusions. Of course, it remains to be seen whether paleoconservatives and national-anarchists alike would agree with that estimation.

An Alternative to the American Empire of the New World Order

Almost childish naiveté, a lack of imagination, simplifications reaching commonness, blind generalizations – these are the impressions one gets after reading Francis Fukuyama's famous essay *The End of History and the Last Man*. Communism's crash in the East and the retreat from the "welfare state" in the West are, in the author's opinion, supposed to mean "the end of history". Humanity has already found its Kingdom of Heaven, which is liberal democracy married to liberal capitalism, and at this point any change or movement becomes impossible and aimless. In his "wishful thinking" Fukuyama is blind to the liberal model's crisis, exemplified by such things as growing electoral absence, the loss of credibility of the great traditional parties[1], and the constant continuance of recession. Fukuyama doesn't want to notice the vitality and dynamism of authoritative free-market systems because this would shake his theory of an unbreakable relationship between parliamentary democracy and the free market.[2] Fukuyama believes in the absolute of the current model of civilization and cannot imagine the existence of humanity in a way different from the technological civilization of economic growth. With the disarming trust of a child, Fukuyama believes that reaching the Paradise on Earth is quite possible (What else would one call "the best possible state of affairs"?).

---

1   In France antisystem parties such as the communists, the ecologists and the nationalists achieved all together 45% of the votes, which is – together with those who didn't vote – the majority of the society. In the USA an unattached candidate, Ross Perot, had a practical chance to win the presidential election; everywhere in the world unconventional parties such as the Belgian ROSSEM or Swiss Auto-Partei are growing in strength.

2   Moreover, it would lead to a suspicion that our well-organized mass society inevitably creates technocratic crypto-totalitarianism!

I guess that is enough of enumerating the new Eternal Happiness Prophet's mistakes. Without a shadow of a doubt, the days of August 1991,[3] although not meaning the end of humanity's history, ended one special age of it. It ended the age in which the major problem was making people happy by fulfilling their material needs, and the most important of the conflicts (whose expression was ideological rivalry between egalitarians and liberals) was attached to distribution of the consumers' goods. However, as soon as the social-statists [adherents of the welfare state] disgracefully stepped down from the stage of history and the free-marketers, as it seemed, triumphed everywhere, the apparent monolith of the "free world" started breaking up again. On a global scale, the "cold war" between the communist East and capitalist West is being replaced by economic occupation of the backward Peripheries by the highly-developed Center.[4] On the internal political scenes, the conflict between the "globalists"[5] and defenders of political autonomy and cultural identity begins to sharpen. There is growing resistance to the self-driving economic growth which, by destroying the natural environment, becomes a threat to the further existence of the human species. Sooner or later these conflicts will find their ideological expression and take the place of the old division between the right and the left wing.[6] New division lines run

---

3   The failure of the coup d'etat in Moscow ended the agony process of communism in its home.

4   "The Center" in my opinion includes highly-developed countries in West Europe, North America and those of the Pacific basin, "the Peripheries" include the majority of the countries of the "Third World". Post-communistic countries have so far been the middle zone, but it is more probable that they will be degraded to "the Peripheries" than promoted to "the Centre".

5   I call "the globalists" a formation which, in the name of economic growth (which would be the key to guaranteeing prosperity for everyone), aims to expand the global market by international integration, which leads to further centralization and cultural homogenization. Another, although not so important, element of the globalization ideology is, in my opinion, the fetish of "human rights", whose defense and spread is also said to be one of the purposes of international integration. (See The New Military Humanism by Noam Chomsky)

6   However, this doesn't mean that the problem of national income distribution has already lost its meaning! It is still very important, especially in the poor countries of the Peripheries.

across the traditional parties. Occurrences that could be noticed during the French referendum concerning the Maastricht treaty can be treated as a standard example: political, economic and cultural elites are quite "pro-globalist" and among ordinary people there is much resistance. The great parties of the center remain the defenders of the "status quo" and at the same time the extreme wings of the political scene are protesting.[7]

New opposition – Resistance to the New World Order – is actually going to develop from the political extremes or, more directly, from those factions of the current right and left wing opposition, which – responding to the challenges of the new reality – will rethink their assumptions. The rest will end up in a Skansen museum of political folklore. The extreme right wing will break into the totalitarians fascinated with a vision of global empire and ethno centrists in whom the devotion to national traditions, autonomy and liberties will win. The same differential process waits for the left wing. The gauchistes[8] have been so far behaving like The Red Army, releasing everyone from everything by force (which has led them into several conflicts not only with the oppressive System but also with different factions of the opposition and the majority of ordinary people). While fighting against national states, they don't notice that above their hitherto enemy grows a new ogre – the supranational super-state that is even less democratic, less responsible to the societies they govern, and more distant from people. Perhaps the left wing, following its old prejudices, will look for an ally against the state, the Church and family in the supranational structures of the Invisible Empire.[9] However, the victory of the Empire over dying national states and traditional communities will be compulsory, because it will put a lonely and rooted out

---

7 In case of Maastricht both the French nationalists and communists voted "No!"

8 "Gauchistes" is a French name I give to all groups from the extreme left wing that was not pro-Soviet.

9 The very same mistake has been made on the part of regionalists (for example, Italian Lega Nord) enthusiastic with the idea of unifying Europe. Actually the "Europe a la Maastricht" won't be a continent of autonomous regions but a satrapy of the Eurobank and Brussels's eurocrats.

individual in front of the monster of supranational techno-bureaucracy. And destroying this Beast will certainly require much more strength than the gauchistes have!

New Alternative: Back to Proudhon

Where is the way out of this trap? What are the requirements for creating New Resistance? Firstly, traditional values such as those rooted in family, ethnic or religious groups have to be rehabilitated (or at least a "non-aggression pact" with the defenders of these "natural communities" should be signed). Secondly, there is a need to accept the rule of self-limitation; self-limitation of people's needs in order to save nature, self-limitation of an individual's freedom in other people's communities or society's favor. Third, and most important, a pluralistic vision of the world, in which ideas and behaviors different from the standards of Political Correctness are on equal terms, also has to be accepted. When fighting for freedom of your own expression, you cannot deny other people this law, even if they are very different from you![10] A pluralistic, decentralized society can be the only alternative to a unified and centralized New World Order, a formless plasma fed on pop-culture. Not only does territorial decentralization (broadening the authority of communities and regions) have to occur but also different cultural communities should gain autonomy.[11] Not only the state but also every community should have the opportunity to proclaim its own laws for its people. In that situation, coexistence of traditional patriarchal families and feminists' or homosexuals' pairs, religious fundamentalists' communities and counter-cultural groups, military-racist communities of the right wing and anarchistic or communistic groups of the left wing would be possible. So that the territorial and cultural decentralization doesn't become a fiction, it has to be accompanied by economic decentralization and that would mean eliminating the concentration of property and

---

10 People's freedom consists also in freedom of their irrational prejudices!

11 Just as in the middle Ages, when ethnic and religious groups and estates had distinct laws and customs, no matter where they lived.

production forms. The information technology revolution gives the opportunity to make this process real. I believe that this idea of a pluralistic society is the only program, which would be able to combine so many scattered and quarrelling sections of anti-System opposition.[12] The only requirement for accepting it is surrendering the ambition of making the whole of humanity happy by your own idea (It will be enough if you concentrate on making yourself happy only). Accepting the variety of the world and the dissimilarity of different people is a task not only for the right-wingers. Otherwise, there will still be the same situation in which a huge silent majority of people are watching scuffles between a handful of left-wing extremists and equally few extremists of the right-wing on TV and the whole show is directed by the elite from behind the scenes.

---

12   In the countries of the Peripheries, the demand for national emancipation from the political, economic and cultural domination of the Center could be an additional (or even the major) link between the left and the right wing opposition.

When the American Empire Falls:

How Anarchists Can Lead the 2nd American Revolution

When I was a kid growing up in the 1970s, I used to hear a lot about the mighty, fearsome Soviet Union, a communist tyranny that was allegedly going to take over the world and, ultimately, invade the United States. There was even a popular film about a Soviet occupation of America, called "Red Dawn", where high school students lead a guerrilla war against the commie invaders. Even as late as 1988-89, when I had since become involved in radical left-wing politics, I used to come across literature from rightist groups like the Christian Anti-Communist Crusade proclaiming the imminent Soviet takeover of the USA. This was the same Soviet Union that had not been able to subdue even Afghanistan, a tiny, impoverished state on the Soviet border in eight or nine years of fighting. Of course, within a few years the Soviet Union fell completely apart and disappeared from the globe.

This will be the ultimate fate of the United States and for the same reasons. Military and imperial overstretch, economic bankruptcy, rising social strife, internal corruption and an expansive police state whose purpose is to maintain the grip of a regime that is losing power; these were the features of the Soviet Union in its final years and it is an apt description of present day America as well. The only remaining question is: When will the US finally fall apart? If the present administration's ambitions for wars with Iran and Syria come into fruition that may well be the beginning of the end. The further the neocon-led Republican Party tries to push its imperial ambitions, the more alienated the regime will become from public opinion. Americans love war, but only if their side is winning. Americans turn tail and run at the first sight of blood on their side. The US is presently losing the war in Iraq and will do even worse in the event of a war with Iran or Syria.

What will happen when the lid finally pops off? The events L.A. 1992 or New Orleans 2005 give us a clue. The present regime maintains power through coercion rather than loyalty. More and more, public loyalty is being transferred to "fourth generation" forces, that is, non-state entities like religions, ideologies, regions and localities, economic interests, gangs and private armies. When the US regime falls, there will be hundreds of factions vying for power in the name of their own agendas. Ethnic rivalries will come to the surface. Despite the "anti-fascist" hysteria of the Left, the primary dangers of ethnic warfare and ethnic cleansing in the future of the US come from the threat of internecine warfare between the various minority groups. The Southwest, in particular, will likely be the scene of a bloody showdown between Hispanics, blacks and Asians. It is unlikely that a "white power" insurgency will emerge from the chaos. There is very little ethnic solidarity among whites, as it has never been necessary, given the historically majoritarian and advantaged position of whites. Also, there is far too much disagreement among whites on other matters. Does anyone really believe that the Jerry Falwell Right and the Michael Moore Left will put aside their differences to follow David Duke into the Aryan Paradise? Most likely, whites will simply flee chaotic areas and take refuge in more remote areas (recall "white flight" from integration in the 1960s and 70s) rather than join the Nazis.

A major military factor in post-System America will be the urban street gangs. Collectively, these groups rival the US military in terms of sheer numbers. In many cities, these are the only groups other than the local government that have any kind of organizational structure, leadership, economic base or arsenal. Gangs will become the de facto governments of many urban areas following the collapse of the state. It is likely that many metropolitan regions will split up into smaller city-states with many of these under gang control. The present day turf wars among gangs generated by drug prohibition are child's play compared to the political rivalries that will emerge when the System falls. Many American cities will look like Beirut circa 1984 or Sarajevo circa 1992 or Belfast in the 1970s. The militia movement that emerged in the 1990s has dwindled a bit in recent years, but will likely rise again in the event of political and economic collapse, societal breakdown or severe social unrest. As the feds disappear, the militias and their support organizations will become the de facto governments of those regions where they are the largest and best organized, primarily rural and heartland areas. Neo-secessionist tendencies have also grown considerably over the last decade. While these are presently still quite small and marginalized they will certainly grow given rising political discontent and systemic breakdown. As for the ethnic factions, separatist or nationalist tendencies like the Nation of Islam or La Raza are among the most popular and best organized factions of the various minority communities. Accordingly, these will emerge as a major force as the system disintegrates.

The post-United States North American continent will be a rather dangerous place indeed. Hundreds of factions will be battling it out in the name of their own agendas. If you want an idea what this will look like, read Tom Chittum's "Civil War Two." The major factions will likely be the various gangs, militias, ethnic militants, secessionists and remnants of the present system. There might also be insurgent forces generated by Stalinist or Maoist elements of the type that currently lead the antiwar movement. There may be leftist militias emerging from the remnants of the anti-globalization movement or from college campus. Many different types of factions, from anti-abortion terrorists to eco-terrorists to theocrats to Marxists, will see the collapse as an opportunity. What will be the opportunities for anti-state radicals? Most so-called "anarchists" or "libertarians" are useless. Both anarcho-leftoids and anarcho-Republicans will be of no value to the struggle whatsoever when the time comes.

These will either be absorbed or eliminated by other factions or they will simply disappear. But what will be the proper course of action for warrior-anarchists?

We should aspire to be everywhere yet invisible. Our model of organization should be that of "leaderless resistance" where we are organized into small, autonomous cells or as lone wolves. These can be either military cells or infiltration cells operating within the context of larger, above ground groups. The focus of our military cells should be to help the present system in its current efforts to commit suicide by feeding it a few extra cyanide pills, so to speak, and to prevent the emergence of a new centralized state structure following the collapse. The focus of our infiltration cells should be to work our way into leadership positions of larger, popular organizations. As the system breaks down, we will use our leadership positions to bring various warring factions together to negotiate a series of settlements where everyone's interests can be accommodated to some degree. This can be done through the application of the traditional anarchist principles of decentralism, federalism and voluntarism. The new system must be organized from the bottom up, where different communities and social groups with different values, beliefs and customs are sovereign in their own enclaves, federated with others when necessary for joint purposes. There are many models for this-the Greek cities, medieval societies, traditional tribal systems, ancient republics, the early American colonies, pioneer societies and contemporary micro-nations. This is the only possible approach to avoiding either chaos or tyranny. We need a revolutionary vanguard of anarchist warriors and anarchist diplomats who can emerge from the disorder to come and provide leadership of an enlightened and progressive nature, just as the US Founding Fathers did in their time and as the Spanish anarchists did during the crisis of the Spanish Civil War. In this manner, we can continue the vision outlined by Jefferson, Paine, Godwin, Proudhon, Bakunin, Kropotkin, Tucker and Rothbard. There is history to be made.

After the Revolution

Some commentators have noted that the imperial arrogance of the American Empire may eventually be its downfall. The USA seems well on its way to becoming bogged down in a very lengthy, protracted war as the economy continues its downward slide. These are, of course, the very conditions that typically signal the collapse of empires. The former Soviet Union immediately comes to mind. If indeed the US were to undergo a political revolution of the type that occurred behind the Iron Curtain some years ago, there would need to be some sort of pre-existing plan regarding what would come after the end of the regime that could be implemented when the day of reckoning finally arrived.

I have repeatedly insisted that local and regional secessionist movements are likely to be the best means of resisting the empire. I have noted the consistency of these with American traditions and the seeds for such a potential resistance are currently being planted in the form of locally-based, grassroots opposition to both war in the Middle East and escalating domestic repression. Preferably, revolutionary forces in various communities should become active and vocal enough that they can effectively gain control over their local county or municipal governments. This could be done through direct political means like electoral action or through more informal means involving the exercise of grassroots pressure on local authorities. There is also the possibility of direct military action in the form of armed insurrection against corrupt local governments by citizen militias. The necessity of establishing an alternative infrastructure prior to formal secession cannot be emphasized strongly enough. Militias must be organized, supplies procured, necessary facilities identified, sustainable communications networks established and indispensable institutions like hospitals, courts and schools maintained in some particular form.

Formal independence from the US regime should not be declared until the revolutionary forces are solidly in control of a majority of the territory of the United States and until credible commitments for aid to the revolutionaries from outside the US have been obtained. Furthermore, a mutual defense pact where each group of local revolutionaries agrees to defend the others will be vital. The state of Vermont or the city of San Francisco will not be able to withstand a blockade imposed by the US military. Although the revolutionary forces should be decentralized in character, the overriding principal of military defense should be "an injury to one is an injury to all". Also, the revolution should be non-ideological in character and devoted to one common objective: smashing the imperial regime and its police state. This does not mean that different elements among the revolutionaries cannot have their own ideological interests. It does mean that sectarian interests of this type must be subordinated to the common struggle. It is precisely this strategy that is working so well for the people of Iraq as this is being written. Apparently, the various components of Iraqi society, including Sunnis, Shiites, Kurds, Christians, Saddam-loyalists, anti-Saddamists and others, have put aside their respective differences in order to combat the Anglo-America-Australian conquerors.

What I will henceforth refer to as the "Iraq Model" provides us with powerful insights into how the federal regime might be effectively combated and defeated. As various geographical areas declare their independence of the regime, there will also be private organizations within other areas that are supportive of the revolutionary cause. Also, sympathy for the revolutionary forces will come from various sectarian and often conflicting ideological forces-patriots, libertarians, Marxists, nationalists, racialists, anarchists-along with persons of "moderate" political temperament and largely non-ideological persons from "mainstream" society. I have written elsewhere of the need for a "revolutionary vanguard" consisting of reasonable and competent persons from various ideological tendencies to coordinate a common resistance effort. I have expressed hope that those in the various anarchist factions who recognize these issues might coalesce into such a vanguard along with persons from other ideological tendencies who think along similar lines. Assembly of a decentralized alliance transcending ideological, cultural and geographical boundaries would be the primary focus of the revolutionary vanguard, for example, in large metropolitan areas leaders of various ethnic nationalist/separatist tendencies, anarchist groups, churches, street gangs, neighborhood associations, business groups, labor unions, et al. might rally their own constituencies behind the revolutionary program and then combine their respective forces into a decentralized political, economic and military force As an illustration, the city of Los Angeles might see the development of a militia federation composed of everything from the Nation of Islam to left-wing anarchists to militant labor unionists to neo-Nazi skinheads to members of the Bloods or Crips to the Baptist or Catholic churches. Development of such forces would probably be more easily done in less densely populated areas where the culture is more homogenous.

Again, it is essential that the revolutionary forces remain focused on the common objective of deposing the current regime. Other matters can be dealt with elsewhere. The rank and file membership of most tendencies, particularly those of a highly sectarian nature, will no doubt be puzzled by the emergence of such disparate alliance. An essential task of the revolutionary vanguard would be for the leadership of each constituency to inspire and motivate their followers to recognize the necessity of such an alliance. What we want is a resistance movement that follows the "Iraq Model" and not the model of Beirut circa 1984 or Yugoslavia circa 1992. In acquiring support from outside the US, it is essential to bypass institutions that are under the control of the US regime or its international allies. For example, some separatist tendencies in the US have attempted to appeal to the UN for recognition. The foolishness of such an approach ought to be obvious enough. The UN is a tool of the US and its First World imperialist allies. Instead, it is best to appeal to nations that resist the international political establishment and to international forces that stand to gain through the destruction of the US regime, whether they are governments or private organizations.

When the time comes that the US regime begins to rumble like the Soviet Union did, much of the US military forces will likely be outside the country fighting World War Three against the rest of humanity. It is quite likely that the draft will have been reinstated by that time. US military forces will be suffering from low morale, high casualties and a shortage of supplies as a result of both economic collapse at home and mismanagement by the military bureaucracy abroad. Riots against war, imperialism and conscription will be taking place with the US, not to mention in other countries, and the regime will respond to this by tightening its police state grip and interring dissenters in concentration camps. Such was the fate of Japanese-Americans in the Second World War. Underground networks of fugitive dissidents will have been formed and the bulk of the leadership of the resistance will likely be operating clandestinely. It will at this point be essential to cultivate a cordial relationship between the revolutionary forces and dissident elements within the state's armed forces. The revolutionary alliance will have to be expanded to include defector units from the US military and auxiliary forces provided by sources outside the US.

As formal confrontation between the revolutionary forces and the state develops, the "Iraq Model" provides us with certain clues as to how the enemy can be effectively defeated. The regimes heavy duty arsenal, its "weapons of mass destruction," will be useless within the domestic US. Resistance forces do not have to "win." They simply have to "not lose." The idea would be to wear down the forces of the state through clandestine guerrilla warfare, sabotage, bombings, assassinations, paramilitary actions and militia self-defense. Machiavelli insisted that the most essential ingredients of an effective fighting force are duty, loyalty and courage. It is precisely these things that the regime's mercenary and conscript forces will be lacking. As Osama bin Laden reminds us:

> "We realized from our defense and fighting against the American enemy that, in combat, they mainly depend on psychological warfare. This is in light of the huge media machine that they have. They also depend on massive air strikes so as to conceal their most prominent weakness, which is the fear, cowardliness, and the absence of combat spirit among US soldiers."

Upon the defeat of the US regime, the first order of business will be to eliminate the machinery of propaganda maintained by the enemy. This will require the direct seizure of enemy media outlets. The revolutionaries should then commence broadcasting propaganda depicting the recently deposed ruling class as a force of unutterable vileness. This should be easy enough to do as it is plainly true. Another matter will be the avoidance of the degeneration of the revolution into internecine fighting between various revolutionary forces or the seizure of central power by any particular faction thereby establishing a new, tyrannical state. This matter necessitates the implementation of radically decentralized social system. Every faction should become sovereign within its own geographical areas. Different communities should be allowed to organize themselves in whatever manner they choose. Large metropolises can be carved up into autonomous districts reflecting the cultural, ethnic or ideological identity of the locals. One town can be a monarchy, the next a democracy, the next communist, the next fascist, or whatever. Sovereign communities could then combine into regional defensive or trade alliances similar to the leagues of free cities that arose during the late medieval period. Different regions could then form a continent wide defense pact against potential future attacks by China, the European Union, etc.

Jump-starting an economy that will have been virtually destroyed is another obvious priority. The first thing that will be needed is a solid currency backed up by some sort of precious metal standard. Local areas can maintain their own currency just as different countries do now. Eventually, competition between local currencies might have a stabilizing and standardization effect and a common currency, similar to the euro, might emerge. Dismantling the vast regulatory bureaucracy that currently stifles certain sectors of the economy will be a priority in the effort to get things moving again. A comprehensive land reform program, whereby state owned land is made available for homesteading by farmers, squatters and others might help to revive the depleted agricultural base in North America. The seizure of industries whose profits are derived from favors granted by the current regime and the conversion of these industries to worker cooperatives might help to restore the industrial base. Medical facilities currently under the control of monopolistic HMOs can be converted to consumer cooperatives.

Matters of crime control and "criminal justice" will largely be an internal issue for individual communities. As much as possible, civilian patrols and informal sanctions should replace professional law enforcement and formal legislation. Communities can simply expel persons who engage in criminal acts. Such persons might eventually find their way to havens of their own. As for the enormous number of Americans who are in prison, a number that will be much higher by the time of the revolution, we might look to the example of Saddam Hussein's granting of general amnesty to prisoners in 2002. All prisoners, excepting foreign spies, were pardoned. Thieves were released on the condition they repay their victims. Murderers were pardoned if the victim's mother agreed. What was good enough for Iraq ought to be good enough for the Americans.

One of the more complicated matters involves the question of what to do with the remnants of the current regime. Those geographical areas where the revolution has not taken root should simply be granted sovereignty and allowed to retain the current system. However, these areas, for obvious reasons, cannot be allowed to possess unconventional weapons. The military-industrial complex should be dismantled, foreign military bases closed, foreign troops withdrawn and the military top brass dismissed from their position and formally retired. Those elements within the state's armed forces who defect to the side of the revolutionaries can continue on as part of the defensive militia of the new system. Other military personnel can simply be discharged and sent home. The entire federal bureaucracy should be dismantled and the buildings that house federal agencies should be sold on the market, opened to squatters and homesteaders or converted to employee cooperatives responsible for earning their own living. Essential services can be converted to consumer cooperatives.

Although local secessionist movements may comprise the base of the revolution, this does not mean that local governments should be retained in their current form. If popular sentiment is overwhelmingly in favor of retaining local administrations, then so be it. But this would not necessarily be wise. Instead, a system of neighborhood autonomy should replace centralized municipal bureaucracies. Local bureaucrats and politicians should be dismissed and voluntary associations should be allowed to take over the administration of local communities. As for the federal regime itself, Congress and the Supreme Court should simply be retired. Particularly troublesome or criminal members of Congress can be exiled to penal colonies. The state's worst criminals are found in the Executive branch of government. Ideally, these would be deported to nations victimized by their imperial aggression to face whatever popular justice may be in store for them or, alternately, handed over to The Hague for trial before a war crimes tribunal.

The new America would be a collection of sovereign regions and communities representing a variety of political, economic and cultural tendencies. We might want to dust off the old Articles of Confederation, perhaps modified, as a means of organizing a common defense and foreign policy apparatus. Upon doing so, the first order of business would be the undertaking of a peace initiative towards those nations under assault by the previous regime and the normalization of relations with those nations. Preferably, a Swiss or Swedish-like foreign policy of neutrality would be adopted. Equitable trade agreements could be worked out with the oil-producing nations. Peaceful relations with the Islamic world might be achieved. And an authentically Jeffersonian America might be an inspiration to citizens of other nations seeking liberation from their own tyrannical states.

The Case for the City-State System

I recently suggested that the next necessary step in the cultivation of the pan-anarchist movement will be the coalescence of the many scattered factions and tendencies within anarchism and overlapping philosophies into a new "Gray" anarchist macro-tribe that maintains its own political and cultural identity in a way that is distinctively independent of the Left and Right or, perhaps more important for domestic U.S. politics, independent of the Red tribe and Blue tribe. At present, far too many anarchists, libertarians, and anti-state radicals retain too great a loyalty to either the Red or Blue, or the Left and Right. While we will continue to draw from both sides of the conventional political and cultural spectrum as our movement continues to grow, the eventually establishment of our own independent identity is a long-term necessity.

I also suggested that we need to identify "wedge" issues that are both compatible with our general aims and outlook but which set us apart from both the Left and Right, the Red and Blue, in a distinctive way, and that opposition to consensual crime laws and the related police/prison state that is built up around these is an obvious choice. The Left will have abortion rights and gay rights, the Right will have gun rights and the pro-life cause, and we will have the libertarian project of abolishing consensual crimes.

I have also discussed the various strategic aspects of pan-anarchism in various detail elsewhere: pan-secessionism, core demographic theory, fourth generation warfare, anarcho-populism, inside/outside strategy, the left-right-center tripartite strategy, a pan-anarchist federation, an third-party alliance, alternative infrastructure, the 25 point platform, building coalitions of anti-state interest groups, a peoples' economic front, legal defense organizations, civilian defense organizations, identitarian organizations, regionalist movements, and a free nations coalition.

I have previously suggested that we pan-anarchists also need to cultivate relationships and strategic alliances with opponents of the system from all over the political, cultural, and ideological spectrum. There are many ways in which anarchism, or at least particular strands within anarchism, overlap with socialism, liberalism, mainstream libertarianism, populism, progressivism, nationalism, traditionalism, and a variety of other philosophies. There are also anarchistic stands within various religious traditions and within the traditional customs of various ethnic communities. Our purpose should be to build an ever-expanding and interlocking network of individuals, organizations, movements, and tendencies that reflect libertarian, decentralist, or anti-authoritarian values.

However, in the process of advocating for pan-secessionism as a meta-strategic concept, it will be easy enough for our positions to be confused with those who hold to a less radical position, such as constitutionalists, states' rights conservatives, and Tenth Amendment advocates. To some degree, this is a good thing. These less radical positions might well be a gateway to positions more like our own for many people. Not everyone is born to be a revolutionary. Some have to be cultivated. Further, we should certainly be capable of engaging in respectful dialogue with those from these less radical tendencies that have not yet reached the same conclusions as ourselves, and we should support their efforts where appropriate.

Yet there is a certain danger in being associated with more conventional forms of decentralism. The principal danger is that it dilutes the radical nature of our message. We are revolutionary anarchists, and not merely reactionary anti-liberals. The second danger is that it risks having pan-anarchism become overly identified with the rightward end of the political spectrum given that states' rights, constitutionalists, and Tenth Amendment advocates are drawn from the Right most of the time. This does not mean that we should seek to create a leftist identity for pan-anarchism. Far from it. As I said above, we need to establish an independent identity of our own. Besides, there are certainly secessionist, regionalist, or decentralist tendencies that trend leftward rather than rightward like Cascadia or the Second Vermont Republic.

The relationship that pan-anarchists should cultivate with the conventional Left, Right, and Center is certainly a unique one. As anarchists and radical libertarians, we are historically on the far left end of the political spectrum. However, our advocacy of secession, decentralization, anti-statism, and anti-totalitarian humanism tactically serves to place us on the right end of the spectrum within the context of domestic U.S. politics. Yet, our advocacy of a left-right progressive-conservative libertarian-populism ends up placing us in the radical center.

While all of these are important considerations when it comes to questions involving both strategy and creating an independent identity for ourselves, there is still the question of formulating effective means of communicating our message to dissidents everywhere and to the wider public. If we do not wish to be identified with the overly conservative positions associated with states' rights, constitutionalism, or the Ten Amendment, it is also practically disadvantageous to attempt to identify ourselves merely with the "anarchist" label, and even more disadvantageous to identify ourselves with some hyphenated or sectarian anarchism term such as anarcho-syndicalism, libertarian municipalism, anarcho-capitalism, and the like. For most people the term "anarchist" is not a political term but a term connoting chaos, and the many hyphenated labels represent arcane or esoteric theoretical concepts that would be incomprehensible or even unpronounceable to most people.

Therefore, we need a simple term with which to signify our ideas that connote our wider decentralist and libertarian values, but are comprehensible on a lay level and linguistically comfortable.

The most obvious means of achieving this goal would be to publicly promote ourselves as advocates of the city-state system. This is an easily understandable idea that also separates us from conventional political rhetoric while simultaneously allowing us to maintain a fully revolutionary, oppositional stance. Advocacy of dissolving centralizing nation-state systems into decentralized city-state systems is certainly a radical position and has revolutionary implications. Yet it avoids the baggage associated with ideological labels.

Just as importantly, advocacy of the city-state system allows for the creation of a practical framework whereby all of the many quite real ideological, cultural, and political divisions among different sects of anarchists, libertarians, decentralists, anti-statists, and anti-authoritarians can be accommodated. For, example both anarcho-communist Murray Bookchin and anarcho-capitalist Hans Hermann Hoppe have been advocates of the city-state system even though their thought represents widely divergent theoretical and philosophical frameworks.

Equally important, advocacy of the city-state system allows for us to do outreach to many different movements, organizations, and tendencies that are not our allies at present, and might otherwise stand in opposition to many of our views. For example, advocacy of the city-state system allows for us to reach out to the wide spectrum of the dissident or radical right, i.e. people who reject the liberal dominance of the existing state systems and mainstream culture, but who have no hope of reclaiming the state or the wider culture for themselves.

Likewise, advocacy of the city-state system allows for us to do outreach to the radical left, i.e. those on the left who reject not merely the right-wing of the system (such as the Republican

Party) but who reject "the American way" in its entirety. While some on the radical left have expressed hostility to our position due to our willingness to formulate alliances with the radical right, this does not need to always be the case. Instead, we need to educate the radical left about the value of the "good riddance" principle and how our objectives allow for the radical left to achieve its goals of both overthrowing the empire and politically separating itself from the Right.

The city-state system allows us to reach out to many countercultures, subcultures, ethnic cultures, religious communities and others who are persistently or periodically under attack by the state, ranging from rural white Christian gun owners to black nationalists to Third World immigrants to gang members, drug users, and prostitutes to Mormon polygamists, fundamentalist home schoolers, and Christian pacifists who refuse to register for the draft.

Lastly, advocacy of the city-state system allows us to reach out to the masses of politically unaffiliated but dissatisfied people with a new set of ideas that are radical but comprehensible, and to connect with people in other nations and other parts of the world who share concerns similar to ours. The way this might play out in the eyes of the general public might be like this:

"The Right: those folks who want to keep attacking more countries, turn total control of the economy over to big business, and impose their conservative/traditional/reactionary social, cultural, moral, and religious views on everyone else."

"The Left: those folks who want big government sticking its nose into everything, raise taxes through the roof, confiscate the guns of honest people, and persecute people who hold to traditional values."

"The Pan-Anarchists: those weird but interesting folks who want to dissolve the government into independent cities and let individuals and contending groups do what they want."

Beyond that, it's simply a matter of gradually convincing a plurality or a majority of the value of our positions (the way advocates of gay marriage and marijuana legalization did it before us), and while simultaneously organizing for the purpose of resisting repression when the state starts to become effectively challenged.

Law and Anarchism

Anarchist Law: Some Hard Questions

Many would no doubt find the idea of "anarchist law" to be an oxymoron. One of the most common objections to anarchism raised by lay people involves the misperception that "anarchy" would be no more than a free-for-all on the part of brigands and criminals. Informed people know better although some anarchists do profess opposition to "law" rhetorically. However, this is simply a matter of semantics. With the possible exception of certain extreme Stirnerites, nearly all anarchists believe that such acts as robbery, rape and murder should be socially disallowed. It is not my aim here to outline a model for an anarchist crime control system as I have done that elsewhere.[1] Instead, I want to address the broader questions of how anarchist legal institutions might be structured and what the content of anarchist law would be, along with the thorny matter of the presence of non-anarchist or non-libertarian ideological or cultural groups in a predominately anarchist society.

Unfortunately, the classical anarchists left this area of their respective ideological systems quite underdeveloped. Proudhon, Bakunin and Kropotkin each indicate in their scattered writings that the inviolability of contracts would serve as the basis of an anarchist legal order.[2] Each of these classical European anarchists claimed to oppose "The Law" as an institution. Yet each of them hinted that something similar to common or customary law would replace formal statist legislation following

---

1   See my *Dealing With Crime In A Free Society*

2   *Anarchism: Exponents of the Anarchist Philosophy* by Paul Eltzbacher

the demise of the state. Something akin to the modern libertarian notion of the "non-aggression axiom" is implicit in many of their comments on these matters. It is important to remember that Proudhon, et al. came out of what was largely a feudal society and were heavily influenced by continental European and, to some degree, classical Greek conceptions of justice, freedom and the like. The Anglo-American notions of individualism were largely absent from their culture. Some of their ideas in this area seem a bit muddled from the perspective of modern North American libertarian sensibilities.

Contemporary leftist-anarchists are hardly any help on these matters. The more articulate and thoughtful persons among their ranks generally claim to favor a social system that resembles nothing quite so much as a New England town meeting combined with economic arrangements closer in form to the Israeli kibbutzim than anything else with a prevailing egalitarian-humanist-multiculturalist-feminist-ecologist-gay liberationist-animal liberationist cultural ethos. I see nothing inherently "wrong" with this model although the way it is described it often sounds more similar to old-style British Fabian municipal socialism than any sort of actual anarchism. "Anarcho-social democracy," as I call it.[3] *(3)* On one hand an America composed of hundreds of miniature Swedens might well be preferable to the current system (at least World War Three would not be looming).[4] However, given the fractiousness of left-anarchist groups, I doubt their ideal of "consensus-based direct democracy" could maintain much of an actual consensus for long. Also, given the infatuation with neo-Leninist "political correctness" displayed by many in this milieu, I suspect "direct democracy" would more closely resemble a synthesis of a Maoist self-criticism session and outright mob rule. Perhaps mob rule at the neighborhood level would not be all that pernicious.

---

3   See my "Anarchism or Anarcho-Social Democracy?

4   Lest I be accused of socialist bias, let me say that I would also consider an America composed of hundreds of Hong Kongs to be an improvement over the current system.

Not surprisingly, it was the American anarchist Benjamin R. Tucker who had the most well developed conception of law of any of the classical theorists. His ideas on these matters were quite similar to those of modern free-market anarchists and, indeed, Tucker was a major influence on Murray N. Rothbard. Tucker did not reject "law" per se and accepted the possibility of prisons, torture and even capital punishment under an anarchist legal system. He seemed to favor something akin to common law juries and regarded what is now called "jury nullification" as the primary safeguard against potential oppression by legal institutions. Rothbard developed the idea of free market law much more thoroughly and modeled his system on non-statist legal codes from the past-Roman private law, medieval Law Merchant, admiralty law and British common law.[5] Rothbard's views on the proper application of libertarian law could be rather doctrinaire and the British classical liberal writer Geoffrey Sampson once speculated that Rothbard probably would have considered any deviation from his system to be a form of crypto-statism to be suppressed by force.[6]

Other anarcho-libertarian legal theorists including David Friedman, Bruce Benson, Randy Barnett, Morris and Linda Tannehill, Jarrett Wollstein, Hans Hermann Hoppe and George H. Smith have attempted to outline models for potential anarchist legal systems. Typically, this will include some scheme where private insurance agencies are the primary providers of crime control or "law enforcement" services with legal institutions resembling the private arbitration services currently in existence. This perspective seems to me to be as legitimate as any. However, critics of these schemes who suggest such a system might more closely resemble a form of industrialized feudalism than anarchism do not seem to be without some justifications for their arguments. Also, it should be remembered that one of the things that caused the anarchical Icelandic Commonwealth to

---

5   *For A New Liberty* by Murray Rothbard

6   *An End of Allegiance* by Geoffrey Sampson

drift into statism was the securing of a monopoly over protection services by a handful of individuals or families.[7] Randy Barnett suggests that "Rights-Maintenance Organizations" might provide protection services in the same way that HMOs currently provide health care. However, HMOs are to a large degree oligopolies made possible by state intervention and the rate of consumer satisfaction with HMOs does not seem to be particularly high.[8]

A number of other possibilities exist. Some in the militia-patriot-constitutionalist movement have sought to set up "common law courts" as a parallel to the state's legal system. There are some fairly solid ideas to be found in this milieu-opposition to victimless crimes, jury nullification, an emphasis on self-defense and victims' rights, an implicit free market economy. Critics have expressed concern that such a system might result in vigilante violence and private lynching. Vigilantism is over-criticized in my view, and vigilance committees often served as a rather effective and beneficent force in the Old West and other frontier societies, yet the legacy of racist lynching and mob action at certain points in the history of the US is unfortunately still with us.[9] The model of "participatory democracy" practiced by the ancient Athenians is sometimes praised by modern anarchists and libertarians.[10] However, a closer look at the actual social structures of Athenian society shows a self-indulgent aristocracy that kept most of the population as slaves, relegated women to a similar status as that imposed by the Taliban and practiced military aggression against neighboring city-states and on the Mediterranean with its superior navy. The Athenian practice of choosing "leaders" through a random drawing of lots might be an interesting model to draw from, but it should also be remembered that it was Athenian democracy that sentenced

---

7   Anarcho-Iceland, from the Ludwig von Mises Institute

8   *The Structure of Liberty* by Randy Barnett

9   *Gunfighters, Highwaymen and Vigilantes* by Roger McGrath

10   London *Spectator*

Socrates to death, thereby souring his successors Plato and Aristotle on the very idea of democracy.[11]

Many traditional societies maintained a system where village or tribal elders were called upon to arbitrate or adjudicate disputes among members of the community but, as the anarchist anthropologist Harold Barclay points out, such systems amounted to a gerontocracy more than anything else.[12] An anarchist society could theoretically develop a type of hereditary system whereby those trained in the mediation of disputes passed their skills and their position down through their line of descendants or where specially trained communities of scholars, kind of like medieval monks, served as ultimate legal authority. However, it should be easy enough to recognize that such arrangements could become the foundation for a caste system that could eventually evolve into a formal state. Coming back a little closer to institutions with which we are most familiar, a network of "protection and arbitration" cooperatives, modeled on contemporary neighborhood committees, homeowners' associations and neighborhood watch programs, could potentially replace the state system. Yet neighborhoods and small towns alike are frequently known for their clannishness and intolerance of outsiders or non-conformists.

It appears that virtually any alternative to the modern state one can conceive of is not without its flaws. This in no way diminishes the viability of the anarchist critique. I believe any one of the models outlined above would be an improvement over the current police state and gargantuan bureaucracy. Even a return to blood feuds, dueling and formal bribery of the type still practiced in some remote areas of the world would not be particularly unattractive when weighed against the status quo.[13] The current system is an

---

11   Of course, it needs to be recognized that decentralized Athenian participatory democracy had little in common with "mass democracy" of the modern corporate statist variety.

12   *People Without Government* by Harold Barclay

13   Tribe Still Means All In Afghanistan by Charles Lindholm March 31, 2002 *Richmond Times-Dispatch*

abomination that all decent people should vehemently oppose. The US maintains the world's largest prison population, with the worst prison conditions of any industrialized nation. Most of these people are imprisoned for "offenses" that are entirely arcane, esoteric, archaic or victimless. The US is second only to China in the number of its citizens it executes annually, many of them no doubt wrongfully convicted. When Republican governors begin commuting the sentences of death row inmates and even some law and order "conservatives" start to come out against capital punishment, we know something is seriously wrong. Murders of unarmed civilians at the hands of the police have become routine. Under the guise of the "war on terrorism", a parallel totalitarian legal system is being created along Orwellian lines. Compared to what the future likely holds, a system of neighborhood-based mob rule, feudatories run by private defense insurance agencies or local gerontocracies with occasional vigilante lynching would be a veritable paradise.

Whatever the structure of anarchist legal institutions might be, this has nothing to say about the content of anarchist law itself. This would likely be a source of considerable controversy if the anarchist "movement" were to continue to expand. Most free market anarchists hold to some variation of the non-aggression axiom: "No one may initiate force against the person or property of another." Immediately the conflicts between leftist and market anarchists become apparent. Many leftist anarchists consider virtually all forms of private property ownership to be a form of violence. I suspect many of these people would also regard any act or even opinion that could be construed as racist, sexist, homophobic, et al ad nauseum to be the equivalent of a violent crime as well. Leftist anarchist communities of this type would likely be enclaves of politically correct totalitarianism. As for other anarchists, there is the matter of defining "initiating force" and property rights. Most anarcho-libertarians recognize the right of self-defense but how far are self-defense rights to be expanded? Is a "preemptive strike" against someone who has repeatedly made credible threats but has yet to act ever justified?

If someone murders a member of my family am I allowed to retaliate in whatever way I choose, or do I have to call the local protection cooperative or defense company, and summon the offender to a common law court? If someone threatens me with their fists am I allowed to defend myself with a gun?

As for the question of property rights, most libertarians favor defining such rights according to the dictates of John Locke or Murray Rothbard. This seems to me to be fairly arbitrary. The idea of property rights defined according to traditional usufructuary principles (occupation and use) seems equally valid. Why not define property rights according to the ideas of Henry George or Hilarie Belloc or Peter Kropotkin or G. B. H. Cole or Ronald Coase or, for that matter, Karl Marx or Gregor Strasser? What about property currently owned by the state or by "private" groups whose ownership is derived from state intervention? Who will receive the title to "public" roads and highways following the demise of the state? Private road maintenance companies? A motorists' cooperative? Will neighborhood associations obtain the rights to streets in their own precinct? Will individual homeowners receive exclusive rights to the sidewalk in front of their residence? What about state-owned industries? Will these be taken over by the workers, sold to bidders on the market or forfeited to creditors? What if the creditor is a state-supported bank? Will government buildings and facilities become the property of former government employees, opened to squatters and homesteaders or turned over to organizations of those who consume their services? Can a village or community claim the right of "common property" to certain resources?[14] Can corporations originally created or chartered by the state continue to claim property rights following the demise of the state?

Controversial social issues are equally difficult. The matter of children is particularly tedious. Is there going to be an "age of majority"? If so, what? Can runaways be forcibly returned to their

---

14   Carlton Hobbs, for Anti-state.com

parents? Until what age? Can parents sell their children to other families? Are sexual relations between adults and children going to be legally prohibited and, if so, what will be the age of consent? Can parents be held legally liable for the material neglect of their children? Would this not be a forcible redistribution of wealth? Can a man impregnate a woman and then refuse to provide any support for the resulting child? Do fathers have equal custodial rights to their children or are children the sole property of their mothers? Is abortion aggression or is a woman who desires an abortion simply exercising her property rights over her own body? Should animals have any legally enforceable protection? Or should even gratuitous cruelty to animals be beyond the reach of the law? How are criminals to be handled? According to the paradigms of retribution, restitution, restoration, rehabilitation or some combination of these? Is there ever going to be capital punishment? Is mercy killing ever acceptable and, if so, under what circumstances? Is drunken driving an act of aggression if no one is actually harmed? Has a crime taken place if someone attempts murder but fails to kill or even injure their intended victim? Is blackmail a form of extortion or the simple acceptance of payment for withholding information? Are acts of "consensual violence" such as dueling or Roman-style blood sports akin to "victimless crimes" such as drug use or prostitution or are these activities something entirely different?[15] If someone sells me a television set I know is stolen am I a participant in a theft or an honest buyer of merchandise whose source is not my responsibility? Is "mental incompetence" ever a legitimate defense on the part of those accused of a crime? Of course, environmental problems provide many unique difficulties of their own.

More complications arise when the matter of the presence of "authoritarian" cultural or ideological groups in an anarchist society are figured into the equation. David Friedman speculates

---

15 Some libertarians argue that dueling or gladiatorial competitions involve an alienation of the self and the "right to life" and cannot be consented to just as voluntarily agreed upon slavery contracts cannot be consented to as they involve alienation of the will. Personally, I find this logic highly questionable.

that anarchist legal institutions could even generate drug prohibition laws if public support for such laws was overwhelming enough.[16] For reasons I will explain, I tend to be skeptical of this claim. However, it is quite likely that local communities would form that would enforce their own cultural, moral, philosophical or religious norms within their own ranks. These could include not only anarcho-socialists, anarcho-syndicalists or anarcho-capitalists but also anarcho-conservatives, anarcho-theocrats, anarcho-nationalists, anarcho-white separatists, anarcho-black nationalists or anarcho-monarchists (yes, all of these actually exist). Additionally, there would likely be territories or enclaves dominated by communists, nationalists, Nazis or theocrats as well as remnants of the present system. There might even be localities controlled by overtly criminal organizations. For example, sections of urban areas might come under the control of gangs following the disappearance of the state. Even this might not be wholly undesirable.[17] Tribute rates tend to be lower than tax rates. I once met an anarcho-Satanist who insisted that in a stateless society contract murder and car theft would become legitimate, respectable professions. While it is theoretically possible that mafia-like organizations might develop their own courts and "defense" organizations that did not recognize their favorite forms of aggression as crimes, such groups of outlaws would still be opposed by nearly everyone else and would find themselves in a state of perpetual war against the rest of society.

At this point, one might be tempted to argue that the kind of pluralistic anarchism I have described here could end up more closely resembling Beirut circa 1984 than any sort of social system conducive to freedom, prosperity and peace. However, I doubt this would be the case. The ideas of decentralization and voluntary association that are central to anarchist thought

16   *The Machinery of Freedom* by David Friedman

17   I am widely criticized for holding the view that street gangs are a bulwark against the state. I once saw a Chicago police official on television saying that many of these gangs view themselves as independent nations at war with the government. I see no difference between them and secessionist movements in the US who are not necessarily libertarian but whom many libertarians nevertheless support as a decentralizing force.

imply that those with common beliefs and values will naturally drift towards one another and engage in mutual self-segregation with those whose views are incompatible with their own. We see elements of this even in the current system. Some states have capital punishment, others don't. Gambling is legal in some localities and illegal in others. The "age of consent" is thirteen in some states and eighteen in other states. Some remote counties even continue alcohol prohibition. The primary disadvantage of decentralization is the persistent threat of tyranny of the majority. Kirkpatrick Sale notes that is will always be difficult to be the black in the white supremacist community, the Nazi in the Jewish community or the atheist in the fundamentalist community.[18] The antidote to this problem is the relative ease with which persons who is outcast in a particular community can migrate to a more hospitable community, or perhaps form their own community, in a decentralized system.[19]

To some degree, the current international system is a "state of anarchy." America, China, Saudi Arabia and the Netherlands all have radically different cultures and social systems. Yet persons from each of these nations regularly travel to other nations and maintain personal or business relationships with others of completely different belief systems or cultural backgrounds. Secular, democratic, capitalist America regularly exchanges people and goods with theocratic, monarchical, feudal Saudi Arabia. I suspect that a particularly effective anarchist method of eliminating the persecution of some social groups by others would be the abolition of state-organized, tax-funded police, courts and prisons. Under the present system, the state seeks to expand its power by aligning itself with private power groups seeking to use the state to repress their ideological, cultural or economic competitors. The "process costs" and "enforcement costs" of such state actions are then passed on to the whole body of taxpayers and distributed throughout society as a whole.

---

18   The 'Necessity' of the State by Kirkpatrick Sale in *Reinventing Anarchy, Again*

19   The Green Panthers, a drug war resistance group, favors establishing a "stoner homeland" in the marijuana farming regions of northern California and southern Oregon.

When this avenue is closed off, those seeking to attack others will simply have to pay for such efforts themselves. No matter how much some people may disapprove of guns or drugs, how many of them would be willing to pay the salaries of DEA or ATF agents out of their own pockets? Economic incentives would likely restrict protection services and legal institutions to the chores of settling interpersonal contractual or common law disputes and the repression of serious crimes. Consensual activities and even some "petty" crimes would largely be ignored or handled by means of informal sanctions. For example, the simple apprehension and expulsion of shoplifters from retail outlets without formal legal prosecution. Coercive enforcement of cultural mores would largely be impossible beyond the neighborhood level.

Hayek concluded that the hallmark of totalitarian law is not so much its brutality as much as its arbitrariness. This describes the legal regime that currently rules over us rather aptly. Orwell once remarked that the perfect totalitarian state would be a formal democracy where thirty percent of the population lived directly or indirectly off of the government. This too has a ring of familiarity about it. The only good thing about Leviathan states is that they eventually collapse under their own excess weight. When the American Empire finally dissolves, perhaps pluralistic anarchist law will be given a chance to thrive.

The Politics of Keith Preston

A reader writes asking me to briefly describe what my own political views actually are. My views are rather complicated and are certainly outside the paradigms and narratives that most people are familiar with. It's rather difficult to attempt a brief description of all that but here's a try:

I consider anarchism, libertarianism, and anti-state radicalism in their myriad of forms to be an evolving form of generalized political radicalism in the same way that classical liberalism evolved in the 17th and 18th centuries and classical socialism evolved in the 19th and 20th centuries. I consider these modes of thought rooted in critiquing and opposing the state to be the probable next wave of radicalism that continues the trajectory rooted in Enlightenment rationalism, liberalism, and socialism.

This evolving anti-state radicalism in its mature form will have the same relationship to the Left that classical socialism had to the classical bourgeoisie. Just as 19th and early 20th century states were a hybrid of feudalism and capitalism, an overlap of traditional society (the "old order") and liberalism, modern states are a hybrid of capitalism and socialism (liberalism fused with social democracy and the managerial revolution). Just as the historic socialists, like Marx, regarded the liberal bourgeoisie rather than the conservative aristocracy (which was a dying force) as their primary enemy, I regard the historic Left (which is now the status quo in all Western industrialized countries) as the primary enemy as opposed to the historic bourgeoisie, "conservatism," or, in the case of the USA, the dying traditional WASP elite.

Just as classical socialism was a myriad of sects and philosophical tendencies that eventually coalesced into a political mass movement, the varying sects and philosophical tendencies that today comprise the anarchist, libertarian, and anti-state milieus will eventually coalesce into an actual mass movement. We see some of that in a very embryonic form at the present time.

Theoretically, I'm a synthesist in the tradition of anarchists like Voline or an "anarchist without adjectives" like Voltairine de Cleyre who favors creating a united revolutionary front of anti-state radicals from across the sectarian spectrum on the model of Spain's historic FAI. This anarchist front will then fill the role of what Bakunin called "principled militants" who are the leadership corps of a much larger populist movement with an anti-state, anti-imperialist, and anti-ruling class orientation. In North America, this radical populism would be oriented towards organizing what I have elsewhere identified as the "ten core demographics" that would be our natural constituents and the vast array of anti-state or marginalized political, social, and economic tendencies I have identified as part of the "liberty and populism" strategy. The primary tactical position of this anarchist-led anti-state populism movement would be what I called "pan-secessionism" i.e. secession by regions, cities, towns, and communities from centralized national regimes and the global plutocratic order in a way that cuts across conventional cultural, economic, ethnic, religious, linguistic or political boundaries. As no state steps down without a fight, the anarchist and anti-state revolutionaries will eventually need to achieve victory through "fourth generation warfare" i.e. an insurgency on the model of groups like Hezbollah or the Peoples War Group.

While the strategy outlined above was designed primarily for North America, some modified variation of it as well would likely be applicable in the struggle against other states and empires, i.e. the EU, PRC, etc.

Beyond this very general task of overthrowing states, empires, and ruling classes, there are also many other secondary or wider projects to pursue, of course. These include creating an alternative social infrastructure that will replace the functions currently assumed by the state (e.g. health care, social services, education, transportation, and et. al.), alternative economic arrangements to replace business corporations, state bureaucracies, and the international financial apparatus, and many single-issue and population-specific tasks to engage in.

Note than none of this has anything to do with wider philosophical orientations. While I am a Nietzschean, there are many others with politics similar to my own who are Kantians, Lockeans, Hegelians, utilitarians, contractarians, implicit Marxists, or who have some kind of religious or mystical perspective.

Nor does any of this have anything to do with specific opinions on contentious public issues like abortion, the death penalty, immigration, religious beliefs, sexual morals, race relations, gender norms, animal rights, etc. There are anti-state radicals on all sides of these kinds of issues. My view is that disputes of this type should be handled by invoking the wider anarchist principles of individuality, decentralization, federalism, mutual aid, and free association. This means that social, cultural, or moral conflict should be a matter of individual freedom, free association to form groups of individuals with like minded values, pluralism, and peaceful co-existence to the greatest degree possible. To the degree this is impossible (for instance, there's no reconciling the views that abortion is child genocide or that abortion is a sacred inalienable right), we should invoke the principles of decentralization, secession, local autonomy, and mutual self-separation of those with irreconcilable differences (like a divorce).

An Interview with Keith Preston

This is an interview I recently gave to a journalist who is writing a book on political undercurrents in the U.S.

Can you tell me a little bit about the American Revolutionary Vanguard and what it stands for?

American Revolutionary Vanguard was founded in the late 1990s by a coalition of anarchists in the North American anarchist movement who wished to pursue a different direction from what was the norm among anarchists in North America at the time. The rest of the anarchist movement was usually oriented towards promoting one of three perspectives: countercultural lifestyle concerns (ranging from veganism to alternative sexuality to squatting to punk music and bicycling), or a kind of clichéd ultra-leftism of the kind that had been developed by Marxist-Leninist and Maoist tendencies within the New Left (such as an emphasis on "white skin privilege" and radical feminism), or old-guard anarcho-syndicalism that had been influenced by early twentieth century syndicalist tendencies such as the Industrial Workers of the World.

We wished to pursue an entirely new direction which would be oriented towards uniting all forms of anarchist, decentralist, libertarian, anti-state, and anti-authoritarian thought around the common purpose of abolishing the state and decentralizing power towards the level of the natural community, and forging a society-wide consensus for this purpose. Much of what we did at the time was a bit tongue in cheek as well. For example, our original name, American Revolutionary Vanguard, doesn't really mean anything. The word "vanguard" is something of a taboo in anarchist circles because of its association with the Marxist-Leninist idea of the "vanguard party." So we always claimed we were trying to reclaim the good name of the word "vanguard." Ironically, back then many in the anarchist milieu were suspicious of us and thought we were Communists, but now we're more likely to be mislabeled as fascists. But the original purpose of American Revolutionary Vanguard was the same as it is now: the formation of an anti-state front.

Can you explain a bit about pan-secessionism and what it means to your philosophy?

Pan-secessionism is a tactical concept that involves the actual application of our philosophy to real world political events. Simply put, our goal is for smaller political and economic units to secede from larger ones. State and provinces would secede from national governments, and cities and communities would secede from states and provinces, all the way down to the neighborhood level. "Power to the neighborhoods" is a common slogan we like to use towards this purpose. Presumably, there could be a parallel economic secession where local and regional branches of industries and managerial units secede and begin to practice autonomy and self-management as well. The concept of pan-secessionism has its roots in two basic ideas. One is the idea of political secession in the form of regional or local autonomist movements such as those currently found in Scotland, the Basque and Catalan regions of Spain, in multiple regions of the US, in Palestine, Tibet, Chechnya and many other places. In the United States, this is a particularly relevant concept given that the United States was essentially founded as a secession of the original thirteen colonies from the British monarchy.

The other idea which has influenced the concept of pan-secession is the old anarchist idea of the "general strike." The notion behind the general strike is that workers establish control over production by means of a mass strike that turns into a popular revolution.

The old anarcho-syndicalist labor organizations like the IWW and the IWA used to advocate for this idea in the era of classical anarchism. However, the concept of pan-secessionism takes this idea much further and advocates a general strike not just in the industrial sectors, but a popular strike against the state and its institutions altogether in the form of regional and local secession, a labor strike, a tax strike, a tenants' strike, a students' strike, and a military strike, in such a way that ruling class institutions are completely undermined.

In certain segments of our population it is cool to say that one is an anarchist. I know some people that call themselves "anarchists" but yet pay their taxes, follow established laws, and generally do what the government tells them to do. Is it possible to be an anarchist and also follow the established rules of one's government?

Anarchism is a philosophy that advocates for the abolition of the state, not a prescription for how one should live within the context of a state-saturated society. Some anarchists choose the route of becoming what have been called "illegalists" and act in open defiance of the state and its laws and commands. Others prefer to live within the system and work for more piecemeal reforms, or simply try to obtain the maximum degree of individual or collective self-sufficiency possible given the circumstances. No one way is the correct way. Instead, it is best for there to be different kinds of anarchists working to undermine the state in many different ways. There are many different ways in which anarchists go about fighting the state. At present, some anarchists in the Kurdish region have formed militias that are involved in direct armed resistance to ISIS and have formed a quasi-anarchist community in Rojava. Other types of anarchists have formed intentional nations like Liberland, and others are working through unconventional political parties like the Pirate Party, and still others are engaged in direction action around such concerns as environmental preservation. The best approach for anarchists to take towards these questions would be to let a thousand flowers bloom.

An Interview with Keith Preston

It is obvious to most thinking people that our current system is way too wrong to last, but still the vast majority of people do not take anarchy seriously. What are today's anarchists doing wrong? What needs to happen to change that? Is there a place for violence?

Most people are not anarchists because anarchists have not yet succeeded at the task of educating others about anarchism to the degree necessary for a popular consensus in favor of anarchism to develop. Our goal should be to grow all forms of resistance until these collectively become a political majority, and then a super-majority, along with the overarching strategic concept of pan-secession and other related ideas. But this is something that takes a great deal of time, and patience is very much in order. The idea that the emperor is to be worshipped as a sun-god did not disappear overnight, nor did the idea of divine right of kings. The false abstractions that are used to justify modern states will not disappear immediately either. However, we as anarchists should be working to undermine and destroy the false pieties that are used to uphold modern states such as the idea of the social contract, the idea that the state is somehow a protector of natural rights or human rights, the idea that the state is somehow based or could ever be based on the idea of popular sovereignty or some kind of mythical general will, and the idea that a mere 51% vote legitimizes whatever a particular state wishes to do.

Instead, we need to promote recognition of the fact that the state is merely a "robber band write large" as St. Augustine said over 1500 years ago. The purpose of the state is to monopolize territory, control resources, exploit subjects, protect an artificially privileged ruling class, and expand its own power. Other claims on behalf of the state are merely evasion and obfuscation. It might be said that the state is merely a mafia with a flag, and a far more insidious institution than the mafia given the much greater level of destructiveness and deceptiveness. Our ambition as anarchists should be to develop a social consensus towards the viewpoint that the state is no more legitimate than slavery or the divine right of kings and other such ills that existed in the past.

As for what today's anarchists are doing wrong, many anarchists have put the proverbial cart before the horse in the sense that their primary focus is on many of the things that we decided were a distraction from the building of a social consensus towards anarchism when we started American Revolutionary Vanguard nearly twenty years ago. Many anarchists have allowed themselves to become absorbed by so-called "progressivism" and consequently are no more effective at challenging the legitimacy of the state than ordinary political tendencies that accept the state as a matter of principle or presumption. Many anarchists are merely activists around popular social issues, or promoting countercultural lifestyles, and consequently have lost sight of the wider picture that involves the need to forge a consensus towards the abolition of the state.

An excess of sectarianism also exists among anarchists. The anarchist movement is largely divided into multiple hyphenated tendencies such as anarcho-communism, anarcho-syndicalism, anarcha-feminism, anarcho-primitivism, anarcho-collectivism, anarcho-capitalism, egoist anarchism, and many, many other tendencies. It would be preferable for anarchists to attempt to find ways to move past these sectarian ideas and find common principles around which anarchists can unite, and common issues through which anarchists can broaden their appeal to larger numbers of people. As for the question of violence, that is a subject on which anarchists do not agree and have never agreed. In the past, there have been anarchists who used terrorist methods to advance their ideals, and other anarchists who are pacifists. I lean towards the idea that different kinds of tactics are appropriate or necessary in different kinds of circumstances.

Another word other than anarchy that gets thrown around without people knowing what it means is "fascist." I have read a few articles that claimed your pan-secessionism tends towards fascism and white nationalism, can you shed any light on that?

Fascism is a concept that has absolutely nothing to do with

either anarchism, as a political theory, or pan-secessionism as an anarchist tactic. Fascism is an idea which proclaims "All within the state, nothing outside the state, nothing against the state" which is how fascism was described by its founder, Benito Mussolini. Clearly, this is the polar opposite idea of anarchism which seeks to abolish the state. Fascism and Nazism are totalitarian ideologies of the Right just as Marxism-Leninism, Stalinism, Maoism, Pol Potism and Kim's Juche Idea are totalitarian ideologies of the Left. But anarchism stands resolutely opposed not only to totalitarian manifestations of the state but to the state in any of its manifestations.

The concept of nationalism is also viewed with suspicion by anarchists because historically nationalism has been used to justify statist oppression, imperialism and inter-state warfare, and nationalism continues to be used for these purposes in some instances. However, there are also people who call themselves anarcho-nationalists, tribal-anarchists or national-anarchists who will affirm the legitimacy of nations, regions, and communities based on a shared culture, language, ethnicity, heritage or religion while denying the legitimacy of the state or the exploitation and cooptation of these things by the state. An example is the way in which the Native American and First Nations tribes, the Australian aboriginals, the Kurds, Tibetans, and many other identifiable population groups are nations but not a state. An even bigger controversy among anarchists involves the idea of whether European or Caucasian ethnic groups can have legitimate claims to identities of these kinds given the past legacy of the European states in perpetrating colonialism, imperialism, the slave trade, ethnic cleansing of indigenous people, apartheid, world wars, and the Holocaust.

While there is strong disagreement among anarchists on this question, I hold to the view that anarchism should recognize the principles of self-determination for all, including all ethnic groups, cultures, religions, nationalities, regions, and communities, and for people of all races, ethnicities, genders, sexual orientations, and lifestyles. There are also anarchist tendencies representing black or African-American anarchists, Zapatista anarchists, native or indigenous anarchists, Buddhist anarchists, Christian anarchists, pagan anarchists, and Islamic anarchists. For this reason, anarchists should give those anarchists who identify with some kind of European ethnicity, culture or religion their seat at the table as well. This the perspective that I believe is most compatible with the ideals of anarchism as a movement that stands in opposition to statism, capitalism, imperialism, aggressive war, and authoritarianism, and which upholds individual liberty, decentralism, voluntarism, federalism, mutual aid, cooperativism, syndicalism, communitarianism, pluralism, human scale institutions, intellectual freedom, free inquiry, free speech, and freedom of association.

The Cat is Out of the Bag

When the future history of the former United States of America is written, the pivotal turning point that likely marked the downfall of the USA will be the events of September 11, 2001.

The United States emerged from World War Two as the most powerful nation-state in the world, rivaled only by the second-rate Soviet Union. American hegemony and dominance spread throughout the world as the countries of Western Europe became protectorates of the USA, and the colonies of the former European colonial empires in Asia, Africa, and Latin America became U.S. client states.

However the postwar era and the late 20th century were also a time of anti-colonial insurgency, leading the U.S. to get bogged down in the anti-colonial war in Indochina and eventually experience defeat. This had the effect of de-legitimizing U.S. militarism to a great degree. For example, the military draft disappeared after Vietnam never to return, and the U.S. has not embarked on a military effort on the level of Vietnam since.

Meanwhile, the unprecedented levels of economic prosperity that the U.S. achieved during the postwar era began to dwindle by the early 1970s. Multiple factors contributed to this ranging from the growing economic power of trade rivals such as Germany and Japan which had originally been cultivated as export markets by the U.S. following their defeat in WW2, to the rise of neo-liberal economic ideology which has contributed to an increasingly widening gap between social classes in the subsequent forty years. Another was the ongoing growth of the global economy, and the implementation of a variety of economic policies too numerous to mention that have led to either stagnation, inflation, unemployment, excessive credit expansion, or other economic ills. This has been a lengthy and cumulative process that has occurred over a period of four decades, but whose effects were really only seriously realized by the Great Recession of 2007-2008, and the ongoing economic deterioration and class polarization that has occurred since then.

The events of September 11, 2001 were pivotal because they had the effect of luring the United States into two wars that proved to be lengthy, costly and tiresome, with *de facto* defeat being the end result.

These military defeats were being experienced during the same time that the economic downturn was dramatically escalating. Further, the forty year escalation of the domestic police state that began with President Richard M. Nixon's initiation of the "war on drugs" continued to expand into a general war on crime, guns, gangs, terrorism, and other more obscure and seemingly innocuous categories. This had the effect of allowing state repression to grow the point where it began to impact not only traditionally marginalized populations, but strands of "Middle America" as well (particularly the rural gun culture). Meanwhile, incarceration rates have reached record levels in U.S. history and on a worldwide basis.

This has had the effect of de-legitimizing "the system" across the board. Now, every major institution consistently maintains a negative approval rating. Meanwhile, political opposition movements have begun to grow, both in the mainstream society and on the margins. The Tea Parties, Occupy Wall Street, and the Ron Paul libertarian/anti-Federal Reserve movement are examples of mainstream opposition politics. The militia movement, which is now larger than it was during its supposed 1990s heyday, and the recent riots in Ferguson are examples of opposition emerging from the margins. Further, movements with a radically anti-state bent are continuing to grow and develop, including anti-capitalist anarchists, libertarianism in all its forms, the right-wing patriot movement, and the sovereign citizens. All of these movements have grown substantially in the past decade, as have new movements with a serious contrarian stance such as the so-called "neo-reactionaries." Additionally, opinion polls now say that 1 in 4 Americans would favor the development of a secession movement in their region or locality. This is up from 1 in 6 in 2008, and would have been unthinkable 20 years ago.

This is also a time a rapid cultural, generational, and demographic change. Caucasian-Americans, the historic ethnic majority of the United States, are now only two-thirds of the U.S. population, down from 90% a half century ago. Mass immigration will insure even greater demographic change in the future. Same-sex marriage, an unthinkable concept a generation ago, is well on its ways to being legalized in every state and culturally normalized.

Support for military intervention is now at an all time low. The fastest growing religion in America is now non-religion. Opinion polls even indicate that public opinion is turning against the war on drugs. Support for marijuana legalization now has a majority, and opposition to the mass incarceration state is growing on the Left and Right. Meanwhile, domestic political conflict within the U.S. is becoming increasingly hostile, polarized, and lacking in civility. Cultural leftists are becoming ever more fanatical and social conservatives are becoming ever more militant in their opposition. It is unlikely that very many of these trends will be reversed in the foreseeable future (or ever). Perhaps none of them will be reversed.

The result of this situation that is likely to emerge in the years and decades ahead is one where an increasingly diverse society begins to fracture on a very significant level. While U.S. military intervention overseas will likely decrease due to its increasingly cost prohibitive nature and lack of popular support, domestic repression will likely continue to increase.

The wider society will become ever more diverse and multicultural. The prevailing cultural trends will lean leftward in every major area, but the socially and culturally conservative opposition will continue to become increasingly militant, and extremism from the Left will become increasingly prevalent as well. Deep cleavages will emerge in society along racial, ethnic, cultural, religious, and geographical lines. Class divisions will continue to widen and the ranks of the poor, unemployed, and homeless will continue to grow.

The middle class will continue to shrink. Wealth will continue to become concentrated at the top and pockets of Third World levels of poverty will increasingly appear in North America. Meanwhile, millions of young adults will discover that their worthless degrees in cultural anthropology and gender studies are just that...worthless.

More and more adult, middle aged and elderly people will be working in bars, restaurants, retail chains, and fast food outlets. More young adults will be living in their parents' basements, and more elderly people will be living with their adult children.

Meanwhile, everyone will be ruled over by a political class that no one likes or respects. Government will increasingly be seen as oppressive, unreasonable, and incapable of accomplishing anything. Opposition movements will continue to appear both in the mainstream and on the margins. Breakaway movements will continue to pop up in regions and communities as the state continues to lose its legitimacy. Meanwhile, the BRIC axis will be rising on the international level and challenging American hegemony. Then there is the potential impact of pending ecological crises, and various wild cards that will likely emerge from rapid technological expansion.

The cat is out of the bag. Hold on, folks. The roller coaster ride is starting to begin.

The Coming Golden Age of Anarchism

It is not unreasonable to suggest that the decades ahead will witness the unfolding of a golden age of anarchism. What is the evidence for this?

- The most powerful state in the world, the United States, the mother country of the empire, is slowly losing its internal legitimacy and serious political discontent is beginning to rise.

- Antiwar sentiment in the United States is at an all time high. War fever could rise again in the event of a war with ISIS or Iran, an intervention in Syria, or a confrontation with Russia. But none of these scenarios would turn out well for the United States in the long run. Instead, the state would continue to lose its legitimacy and antiwar and anti-imperialist feeling would come back on an even stronger level.

- Class divisions are the widest they have been in a century in the United States. This all but guarantees the re-emergence of class-based politics at some point in the future. Proponents of alternative forms of decentralist economics will then begin to find a ripe audience for their ideas.

- Public opinion is slowly turning against the police state, prison-industrial complex, and the war on drugs. Sentiment of this kind will likely begin to grow exponentially in the future. It is likely that resistance to domestic American fascism will be the civil rights movement of the 21st century.

- One in four Americans are now sympathetic to secession by their region or community, and these sympathies will probably increase as the system begins to deteriorate.

- One in four American adults now has a criminal record due to over criminalization. This can only have the effect of undermining respect for the state and its legal decrees.

- The idea of the state as the savior of humanity is an idea that is coming under increasing disrepute. The fiscal debts alone of modern welfare states likely guarantee their ultimate demise.

- National patriotism is on the decline everywhere in the developed world, and citizens are rarely if ever willing to make sacrifices on behalf of the states that rule over them.

- Traditional forms of out-group hostility are increasingly unpopular and socially unacceptable, particularly among younger people, making it difficult for states to legitimize themselves on the basis of appeals to national, racial, cultural, or religious chauvinism.

- Past liberation movements for traditional out-groups have opened the door for the development of still more liberation movements.

- We are observing in the United States the gradual emergence of a libertarian-oriented "grey tribe" as a third force in opposition to the conventional state-centric "red" and "blue" tribes.

- The rapidly accelerating demographic change in the United States will render it increasingly more difficult for the United States to cohere as a continent-wide centralized regime, and to maintain control over an increasingly diverse society.

- The rise of the fourth generation warfare model is having the effect of undermining the legitimacy of states on a worldwide basis.

- The growing rift between the political class, and the military and law enforcement class, is having the effect of undermining the morale of the latter, and their loyalty to the former. Increased diversity within the ranks of the police and military will undermine the cohesion of those institutions.

- Technological innovations ranging from 3-D printing to crypto-currency will make it increasingly easier to evade the state in a variety of ways.

- The internet is allowing for the proliferation of an ever greater variety of independent media outlets, and is allowing information consumers to have access to an ever greater variety of sources of opinion.

- Anarchist and related or overlapping movements are continuing to grow at a significant pace in part because of the availability of social media and contemporary communications technology.

- Electoral participation continues to continue thereby undermining the legitimacy of the state's coronation process.

- Growing concern about environmental difficulties will increasingly expose the inability of governments and corporations to effectively protect and preserve the environment.

- The adoption of totalitarian humanism as the self-legitimating ideology of the ruling classes will undermine the loyalty to institutionalized authority of those sectors that are normally the most conservative, and most likely to, for instance, join the ranks of the military and the police.

- Very timid opposition or protest movements have already appeared in the form of Occupy, the Tea Party, and the Ron Paulistas. These will be prototypes for much more radical movements in the future.

- The totalitarian humanist ruling coalition is inherently unstable, and ultimately has no unifying thread other than opposition to traditional W.A.S.P. hegemony. Eventually, this coalition will crack due its own internal contradictions.

- The state-centric Left will be increasingly discredited and people who want to rebel against society will ultimately have nowhere to go other than to libertarianism (of some kind) or to fascism. However, fascism maintains a level of social standing that is frequently comparable to that of pedophiles. This is not likely to change in an increasingly diverse society. Therefore, its growth potential is minimal.

- The excesses of totalitarian humanism will likely provoke a right-wing backlash in the future. Such a backlash may well be necessary. However, the prospect of fascists becoming genuinely competitive in Western politics at any point in the future is very remote. Even the populist-nationalist parties of Europe have had to moderate their ideology, rhetoric, and tactics to a great degree in order to obtain electoral legitimacy.

- The excesses of totalitarian humanism are indeed troublesome, but already opposition movements are beginning to rise in the form of such tendencies as the men's rights activists, the dark enlightenment, and the neo-reactionaries. It is highly unlikely that these opposition movements will grow to dominant status, but they may fill the necessary role of obstructing the worst ambitions of the totalitarian humanists. Meanwhile, totalitarian humanism increasingly gives the appearance of being criticized in leftist and libertarian circles as well.

- The appearance of a libertarian-oriented radical opposition movement, or movements, in the United States that eventually brings down the ruling class of the mother country of the empire will have a worldwide ripple effect, and comparable movements will begin to appear in many different countries.

- Anarchism is historically to the left of Marxism. The Marxists dominated radicalism in the 20th century. Now it's our turn.

www.ingramcontent.com/pod-product-compliance
Lightning Source LLC
Chambersburg PA
CBHW061722270326
41928CB00011B/2078